THE
HONORABLE
ELDERS

THE
HONORABLE
ELDERS

A CROSS-CULTURAL ANALYSIS
OF AGING IN JAPAN

Erdman Palmore

1975
DUKE UNIVERSITY PRESS
Durham, North Carolina

to Brydie Palmore
who makes growing older exciting

Contents

Preface and Acknowledgments

The bowl with a gift
of *Kaki*[1] is returned with
origami[2] swan.[3]

The Japanese make it a point of honor to always repay gifts and favors, even if the repayment is only a token one. I cannot hope to repay adequately the many generous services and gracious help that I have been given, both in Japan and in the United States, which have made this book possible. The following acknowledgments of the main institutions and persons who contributed to this project are only small tokens, like the *Origami* swan, of my indebtedness and gratitude.

This book is based on materials and observations gathered in Japan during my sabbatical leave in 1973. My initial thanks, therefore, go to Duke University for providing support during this leave. Travel funds were provided by a Duke Bio-medical Sciences Support Grant (#5-S05-

---

[1]A large sweet variety of persimmon.

[2]The Japanese art of folding paper to represent animals or flowers.

[3]These poems at the beginning of each chapter are in the classic *Haiku* form of three lines, with five syllables in the first and third lines and seven syllables in the second line. *Haiku* also usually contain some reference to a season or the weather. For example, in the above *Haiku*, the *kaki* is a symbol of autumn. All the *Haiku* in this book are by Erdman Palmore.

RR07070-07). Thanks are also due the Duke Center for the Study of Aging and Human Development, the Department of Psychiatry, and the Department of Sociology for allowing me time to study Japanese before my trip to Japan and time to complete the book after my return. Partial support for completion of the book was provided by USPH grant #HD-00668.

Fortunately, Japan has some of the best statistics in the world on their aged population, as shown by the tables in this book. Unfortunately, few of these statistics had been translated into English. Therefore, while it was unnecessary for me to conduct a large-scale survey to secure the needed information, it was necessary to review thousands of tables published by various government agencies and private institutions and to translate several hundred relevant to this analysis.

In order to facilitate this work, the Tokyo Institute of Gerontology generously provided office space and staff assistance. Special thanks go to Mr. Daisaku Maeda and his staff in the Social Welfare Section for providing materials and answering my many questions. Miss Yoshiko Someya spent many patient hours helping me review and translate hundreds of tables. However, any inaccuracies and awkwardness in the translations should be blamed on my limited knowledge of Japanese.

Mr. Mikio Mori, Expert on Aging at the Ministry of Health and Welfare, not only arranged for a series of questions from the Shanas cross cultural survey of the aged to be included in the 1973 Japan Survey of the Aged (in order to facilitate direct comparison with the United States, England, and Denmark), but also was generally helpful in providing me with materials, contacts, sponsorship, and living arrangements.

I cannot list all the people in Japan I have interviewed or who have informally discussed this fascinating topic with me, but my appreciation for their help is not diminished by their anonymity. My students in Sociology at Sophia University made a special contribution to this book through their cooperation in two class projects investigating deference toward the aged and the changing status of Japanese aged.

Preliminary drafts of the manuscript were read and valuable suggestions were made by Peyton Palmore III, P. Lee Palmore, Sr., Jae Jong Kim, Robert Atchley, Donald Cowgill, Mikio Mori, Daisaku Maeda, Yoshiko Someya, and David Plath. My intellectual debts to such theorists as Max Weber and Talcott Parsons will become obvious. Ethel Shanas and Donald Cowgill are the two pioneers in cross-cultural gerontology who have most stimulated my interest in this field. Peyton Palmore and his family helped in innumerable ways to make our visit to Japan productive and a joy we will will always remember.

My wife, Brydie Palmore, contributed the drawings which illustrate my *Haiku* introducing each chapter.

Finally, in a book about honorable elders it is particularly appropriate to acknowledge my debt to my honorable parents, Rev. and Mrs. P. Lee Palmore, Sr. Not only did they have the foresight to give birth to me in Japan and to let me stay there my first six years, but they also have encouraged and fed my continuing interest in Japan ever since.

1
Introduction

*The Honorable
Elders:* golden autumn years
Or empty slogan?

Just as old age is a universal phenomenon, there has been an almost universal increase in the number of older people and in the proportion of the old in the total population. This is an inevitable result of both declining birth and death rates. This increasing proportion, combined with social and economic changes resulting from industrialization, has in turn produced an increase in concern for "the problems of the aged." The problems of the aged are also problems for all the rest of society: the provision of appropriate roles, maintenance, medical care, etc. Furthermore, each of us has a personal interest in aging because, unless we die early, each of us will become an aged person.

Given these facts, the need for better understanding of old age is obvious. Less obvious may be the need for a cross-cultural analysis such as the present one. The need is both theoretical and practical. On the theoretical level, we cannot hope to establish a universally valid science of gerontology until we find out how well our theories about aging and the aged apply in other cultures. On the practical level, our vision of possible solutions to the problems of aging will be unnecessarily limited if we confine ourselves to the preconceptions and limited experiences of our country or even of Western culture. This book is basically an attempt both to broaden the base for the emerging science of gerontology and to enlarge our vision of possible ways to improve the quality of our later years.

The rest of this chapter is a discussion of ways in which we hope to fulfill these purposes through a description and cross-cultural analysis of the aged in Japanese society.

PARADISE OR PURGATORY?

"The honorable elders" is a translation of the most common term used in Japan for the aged: *otoshiyori*. For example, the signs giving priority to the aged and handicapped on certain seats in commuting trains use *otoshiyori*. The elements of this word literally mean "honorable age achieved." The adjective form, *Toshiue*, literally means "age above," or "elder." It is true that in recent times *otoshiyori* has taken on patronizing connotations, but until recently it was considered the most respectful term to use for the aged. Another term is *koreisha*, which literally means "high age person." A third honorific term is *go-inkyo-sama*, which means an honorable retired person. A more neutral term is *rojin*, which combines elements meaning a white-haired and stooped person. However, the fact that the more frequently used terms have respect and honor built into their roots is an indication of the high status traditionally enjoyed by older Japanese.

One of the main purposes of this analysis is to examine the extent to which this traditional respect for the aged continues in modern Japanese society. Some descriptions of the aged in Japan portray them as at the peak of the status and power structure, obeyed and venerated by their children and grandchildren, respected by all of society for their years of experience and accumulated wisdom (Buck, 1966; Benedict, 1946; Hearn, 1955). Some modern writers have implied the opposite extreme: that industrialization and rapid social change have transformed the aged into cast-out, useless relics of the past who are a burden at best and are often a nuisance and obstruction to modern progress and enlightenment (Plath, 1972; Niwa, 1962; Ariyoshi, 1972). This basic question of the present status and social integration of the aged in Japan provides a test of two general theories in gerontology.

MODERNIZATION AND THE AGED

One theory asserts that modernization causes a progressive decline in the status and social integration of the aged (Cottrell, 1960; Palmore, 1969; Cowgill and Holmes, 1972). It assumes that the status of the aged in preindustrial societies (or at least in stable agrarian societies) tends to be high because the aged tend to accumulate knowledge and wisdom through their years of experience and to build their power over land, extended family, government, religious, and other institutions. Industrialization, however, decreases the importance of land as a source of status, decreases the importance of the extended family, increases geographical mobility, and rapidly changes technology, social structure, and cultural values. Other aspects of modernization which theoretically reduce the status of the aged are the increase in urbanization, modern mass education, and the proportion of the aged. As applied to Japan, this theory would predict a relatively low and declining status for the aged.

A similar theory may be derived from the Marxian tradition. Marxian theory asserts that culture and social structure are determined by the economic system and that a person's status is determined by his relationship to the means of production. But in capitalist industrialized societies most aged are retired and have *no* relationship to the means of production. Therefore, the status of the aged in industrialized societies should be relatively low according to this theory. Since Japan is now one of the most industrialized captalist societies, the status of aged Japanese, according to this theory, would be among the lowest in the world.

Max Weber, however, opposed the Marxian theory and asserted that culture can have an independent effect on economic and social structure. For example, one of his main theses was that the Protestant ethic stimulated the rise of capitalism, rather than vice versa (Weber, 1930). Applying Weber's theory of the independent effect of culture to Japan, one might hypothesize that the Oriental tradition of respect for elders would prevent a major decline in the status and integration of the aged, despite industrialization. The evidence in this book will tend to support this hypothesis and therefore is relevant to the more general controversy between economic and cultural determinism. Japan provides a unique "test case" because of its unique combination of modern industrialization with older Oriental traditions.

DISENGAGEMENT

The second general theory in gerontology to which this evidence is relevant is disengagement theory (Cumming and Henry, 1961). Disengagement can occur on three levels: the physical, psychological, and social. Physical disengagement means a reduction in the amount of physical activity, a slowing down and conservation of energy. Psychological disengagement refers to the withdrawing of concern from the wider world to primary concern for people and things directly affecting oneself, a shifting of attention from the outer world to the inner world of one's own feelings and thoughts. It involves the reduction of mental and emotional energy. Similarly, social disengagement means the reduction of social activity and involvement, a "mutual withdrawal or 'disengagement' between the aging person and others in the social system."

Two main parts of disengagement theory have become most controversial. The first part states that disengagement is biologically inevitable as a person ages; therefore most older people, independent of ill health or poverty, in fact do progressively disengage as they become older. The second part states that disengagement is *good* for both the aged and society. It is good for the aged because it is an acceptance of the inevitable decline and death, a conservation of energy, as the best way to adapt to the declining abilities of old age. Therefore, disengaged older people tend to be happier and healthier than those who try to remain more active. Disengagement is good for society because it gradually can transfer the functions previously performed by the aged to the young and thus society can avoid the problems caused by increasing incompetence or inevitable death of the aged.

Both parts of this theory have been widely attacked and defended, with scores of articles presenting evidence and arguments on one side or the other. Suffice it to say here that the weight of the evidence is generally against both parts of the disengagement theory, at least in the unequivocal form stated above. As for the first part, disengagement is not inevitable, except shortly before death, and many older people show little or no overall disengagement (Pal-more, 1969). As for the second part, most evidence indicates that disengaged older people tend to be more unhappy, lonelier, sicker, and die sooner than more active older people (Palmore, 1969, 1971, and 1974).

The evidence from Japan is relevant to disengagement theory in three ways. We will see that: First, the Japanese aged tend to be more active and involved than the aged in other industrialized societies. This helps to show that disengagement of the aged is not altogether biologically inevitable and that the amount of disengagement in an aged population is largely determined by the culture and social structure. Second, in comparing Japan to other countries, this higher rate of activity in Japan is associated with higher average measures of satisfaction and health among the aged. Third, *among* the Japanese aged the more active Japanese are also more satisfied and have better health than the more disengaged Japanese. This suggests that activity, rather than disengagement, tends to promote satisfaction and health.

SUGGESTIONS FOR THE WEST

While Japan is no paradise for the aged, and even though it is often difficult to transplant practices or attitudes from one culture to another, many Japanese practices and attitudes may suggest ways in which the quality of later life in the West could be improved. These range from the simple practice of giving the aged and handicapped priority on certain designated seats in commuting trains to the complex set of attitudes and practices which result in almost twice as many of the aged in Japan being employed as in the United States. This is another purpose of this book: to describe such promising ideas and suggest ways in which they might be adopted in the West.

BASIC DESCRIPTIONS

In addition to the above purposes, the basic social and attitudinal characteristics of Japan's older population will be presented. This is the first time that most of this basic information has been made available to the West. This fact is surprising in view of the extensive and high-quality statistics on their aged. It probably is another reflection of the culture-bound nature of most Western gerontology. Even the pioneering cross-cultural survey by Shanas and her associates (1968) was limited to three *Western* societies. *Aging and Modernization* by Cowgill and Holmes (1972) was the first book to attempt general descriptions of the aged in *all* types of societies around the world. While that book made an outstanding contribution to comparative gerontology, its attempt to survey the entire world meant that little in-depth and quantitative analysis was possible. The earlier cross-cultural work of Leo Simmons was limited to preindustrial societies (1960).

Thus, we hope that the present volume will make a contribution to the growing body of cross-cultural knowledge and theory and will aid in the development of a truly international science of gerontology.

METHODS

There will be a variety of data utilized, both quantitative and nonquantitative. Most of the statistical data on older Japanese comes from a series of surveys conducted by the Japanese Census Bureau, the Ministry of Health and

Welfare, the Prime Minister's Office, and the Tokyo Metropolitan Government. The September, 1973, Survey of the Aged conducted by the Ministry of Health and Welfare contained a series of questions (designed in consultation with this author) to be as directly comparable as possible to the questions used in the Shanas cross-cultural survey of the aged. These surveys are of a high quality, being based on probability samples of at least 2000 persons each. Standard survey techniques of sample selection, interviewing procedure, and data processing were used. Cooperation was high and refusal rates were low, probably because of the ingrained Japanese tradition of following orders from the government (in this case, a "request" by the government interviewer for the respondent to answer the questions in the interview schedule). In all surveys there is the problem of social desirability bias which influences an unknown proportion of responses toward more "desirable" answers; this may be a greater problem in Japan with its emphasis on "saving face". This caution should be borne in mind when comparative survey statistics are presented.

Wherever possible, we compare the Japanese statistics with United Nations statistics on other countries or with results from Western surveys. We also present trend data to analyze the extent of change in the situations of Japanese aged. Thus, the analysis is not only cross-cultural, but cross-temporal as well. In addition, we often use cross-tabulations by sex, age, density of population, education, and health in order to analyze the effects of these factors on the basic statistics. This kind of analysis helps in making inferences about the future, the effects of urbanization, of disengagement, and so forth.

In order to compare the social status of the aged relative

to the non-aged, both over time and between countries, we use the Equality Index (EI). The EI may be described in several ways. It is the proportion of two groups' percentage distributions which overlap each other. Or, it is the sum of the smaller of the two percentages in each category, when two percentage distributions are compared. It can be thought of as the percentage of complete equality, because 100 would mean there is complete identity between the two groups' distributions and 50 would mean that 50 percent of the inferior group would have to move upward to equal the higher group. As used in this book, the lower the EI, the lower the status of the aged relative to the non-aged in terms of occupation, education, or whatever characteristic is being compared.

For example, Table 1-1 presents the 1970 industry distribution of employed persons aged 15-64 and persons over 65. Fewer younger persons were in the primary industries (17 percent compared to 47 percent of the aged), and fewer of the aged were in the secondary (17 percent) and the tertiary industries (36 percent). The EI is therefore the sum of these lesser percentages: 17 plus 17 plus 36, which equals 70. This shows that in terms of industry, the aged were 70 percent similar or equal to the non-aged. To

Table 1-1. Industry of employed persons by age, Japan, 1970 (percentage distribution)

Industry	15-64	65 +	EI
Primary	17	47	17
Secondary	35	17	17
Tertiary	48	36	36
Total	100	100	70

Source: Japan Census Bureau, 1970.

achieve equality with the non-aged, 30 percent of the aged would have to move out of the lower paying primary industries into the secondary and tertiary industries.

There are several advantages of the EI over the other measures that have been used to compare equality between groups: it ranges from a true zero to 100; it can be used with any kind of quantitative data (ordinal, nominal, or interval); it is not subject to the heavy influence of a few extreme cases; it reflects general changes in distribution as well as in central tendency; it is easier to calculate and understand than most other indexes (Palmore and Whittington, 1970 and 1971; Palmore and Manton, 1974).

The non-quantitative methods used in this study include observations of Respect for the Elders Day; behavior of Japanese toward the elders on trains, subways, and other public places; descriptions of public programs for the elders; interviews with gerontologists, with government officials, with older Japanese, and with younger Japanese; reviews of the literature on older Japanese; and illustrations drawn from Japanese stories and novels about the elders.

SUMMARY

The universal increase in the numbers of older persons combined with rapid social change has produced increasing concern with problems of the aged. Cross-cultural analysis of the aged is necessary both to develop a universally valid science of gerontology and to enlarge our vision of possible ways to improve the quality of the later years. A basic question for this book is, "What is the present status and social integration of the aged in Japan?" The answers to this question provide a "test case" for the theory that modernization causes a decline in the status and integration of the aged, and provides evidence opposing the theory of disengagement. Another purpose is to describe those practices and attitudes in Japan which might be useful in improving the situation of aged in the West. Finally, the book provides the basic social and attitudinal characteristics of older Japanese. This is the first time most of this basic information has been made available to the West. We use a variety of methods in this analysis including the Equality Index, cross-tabulations by time, by country, age, density, education, and health, as well as illustrations drawn from observations, interviews, and the literature on Japan.

2
The Setting
and the
Tradition

The Chrysanthemum,
the Sword[1]; old, new; East and West;
blend of many things

A major thesis of this book is that, while the economic system in Japan has become similar to that of other industrialized nations, Japan's distinctive social system and cultural traditions have nevertheless maintained a high degree of integration for the aged. Hence, it is important to establish both the similarity of the economic system to those in the West, as well as the distinctiveness of the Japanese sociocultural system.

MODERN JAPAN

The Japan archipelago spans a range of latitude roughly 30° to 46° north, or approximately the same as New Orleans to Minneapolis. Thus, the climate is comparable to that of the eastern United States, but generally warmer than that of northern Europe, e.g., Britain and Denmark.

---

[1]*The Chrysanthemum and the Sword* by Ruth Benedict is a classic description of the dual aesthetic and aggressive characteristics of Japanese.

The population is about one-half that of the United States, but Japan's population is crowded into one-twenty-fifth the area of the United States (Table 2-1). Japan's population density is thirteen times as great as the United States, although not much greater than Great Britain's. Thus, density cannot explain the large difference between Japan and Great Britain in proportions of the aged living with children.

Japan is one of the most industrialized nations in the world. Her gross national product per capita is about the same as Great Britain's, and her total gross national prod-

Table 2-1. Comparative statistics on Japan, United States, Great Britain, and Denmark (1970-72)

Statistic	Japan	U. S.	Britain	Denmark
Area (sq. mi.)	142,774	3,614,254	94,200	16,629
Population, 1972 (in millions)	107	209	56	5
Density per sq. mi.	748	58	593	302
Percent urban	68	74	77	46
Gross national product, 1971 (billions)	$292	$1,152	$162	$20
GNP per capita, 1971	$2,757	$5,515	$2,877	$3,978
Per capita income, 1971	$2,068	$4,583	$2,356	$3,354
Percent of GNP from manufacturing, 1970	37	27	35	20
Percent of labor force in agriculture, 1970	16	5	2	9
Percent GNP expended on education, 1972	13	8	6	5
Birth rate (per 1000), 1972	19	17	16	15
Death rate (per 1000), 1972	7	9	12	10
National increase (per 1000)	12	8	4	5
Percent age 65 and over, 1970	7	10	13	12

Source: United Nations, 1971; U. S. Bureau of Census, 1973.

uct is second only to the United States (among non-communist countries) despite her relatively small size. Over two-thirds of the Japanese now live in urban areas, which is much more than Denmark but somewhat less than the United States and Great Britain (Table 2-1). More of Japan's gross national product comes from manufacturing than any of the comparison[2] countries. However, a larger proportion of her labor force is in agriculture (16 percent), and her per capita income ($2,068) and per capita GNP ($2,757) are lower than the comparison countries. This is reflected in a lower average standard of living and lower expenditures for retirement pensions and social welfare programs in general.

One reason that Japan is so heavily industrialized is that her capacity to feed her people is restricted by the ruggedness of the terrain. About three-fourths of the country is nonarable, that is, too steeply graded for crop cultivation. Therefore, Japan needs to manufacture enough goods to trade for food and the necessities of modern life.

In order to maximize the crop yield from the limited arable space, Japanese farmers have resorted to various ingenious techniques including producing two crops a year in the southern part of the country, intensive cultivation, heavy use of natural and chemical fertilizers, terracing of upland fields, use of dikes to reclaim marshland, and elaborate irrigation projects.

Animal husbandry has received little attention in Japan, both because of the shortage of pasture land and because meat is a relatively inefficient way to produce food calories. The dairy industry is very small. Animal products

[2]The term "comparison countries" refers to the three industrialized countries used in this book for comparison purposes: The United States, Great Britain and Denmark.

still constitute a relatively small part of Japanese diet, even though meat consumption has more than doubled in the last ten years. Instead, the Japanese derive the majority of their protein from cereals, soybeans and soybean curd (tofu) which have a higher protein content than beefsteak and fish. The average Japanese eats about 65 pounds of fish per year, but only 5 pounds of meat, compared to the average American who eats 12 pounds of fish and 140 pounds of meat (Webb, 1957). Japan has been the world's foremost fishing country for most of this century and accounts for more than one-fourth of the world's fish catch.

Rice is the principal crop because it has the highest caloric value of all cereals. The second largest cereal crop is barley, followed by wheat, soybeans, corn, and several million tons of potatoes. The most important nonfood crops are silk, tea, and tobacco.

In both farming and fishing, older Japanese play a prominent role because younger people have tended to move to the cities and industries, while the older people have tended to stay on the farms and in the fishing villages. We will see that this is related to the high rate of continued employment among the aged (Chapter 4).

Japan has been so successful at industrializing and exporting that she has been one of the few nations with a positive trade balance. In 1970, she exported $19 billion and imported $15 billion (Associated Press, 1973). However, this favorable balance has recently declined with international currency reevaluations and the fuel shortage. Japan is dependent on imports for 95 percent of her petroleum needs. Nevertheless, she continues to be a leading producer of ships, textiles, electronic equipment, optical goods, precision instruments, and motor vehicles.

Almost all Japanese are literate, just as in other industrialized nations, and she spends a relatively high proportion of her gross national product on education (two-thirds more than the United States, and more than twice as much as Great Britain and Denmark). This emphasis on education has contributed to her rapid industrialization and increase in gross national product.

Japan's higher birth rate and lower death rate combine to produce a natural population increase substantially higher than the other three countries (Table 2-1), and this increase aggravates her problems with overcrowding. The 7 percent of the population over age 65 is a lower percentage than in the other countries, but this percentage is increasing with recent declines in birth and death rates, so that it is expected to approximate that of other industrialized countries within two or three decades.

SOCIAL-PSYCHOLOGICAL TRAITS

Compared to the United States and Great Britain, Japan is a relatively homogeneous nation. Racially, most Japanese resemble the Mongoloids of China and northeast Asia, although there is some admixture from the Caucasoid Ainus and Malayans from southeast Asia. The 600,000 Koreans are the only important ethnic minority in Japan.

In feudal times there was a pariah caste called *eta* who performed several of the menial occupations that were taboo to orthodox Buddhists such as slaughter of animals, execution of criminals, and manufacture of footgear. The *eta* caste was theoretically abolished about a hundred years ago and they are now called *burakumin*, but true social equality is yet to be achieved. Intermarriage with *burakumin* is still frowned upon by most Japanese, and the ancient stigma still forces most of them into degrading occupations. However, known *burakumin* are now a relatively small group, and discrimination against them is declining.

Nearly all Japanese (except for one percent who are Christians) are at least nominally Buddhists or Shintoists, or both. This homogeneity may facilitate the integration of the aged because there are few aged who must face the "double jeopardy" of being both aged and in a minority race.

Generalizations about the social-psychological traits of any people are, at best, of limited usefulness for several reasons: usually little or no systematic evidence exists to prove the validity of the generalizations; such generalizations tend to become stereotypes which ignore the many exceptions and variations among real people; such generalizations tend to be couched in value-loaded terms which turn them into criticisms or praise rather than objective description of facts. Nevertheless, a better understanding of the social-psychological setting for this study may be gained by a consideration of some of these generalizations, particularly if one bears in mind the above limitations.

It is often said that Japanese display unusually strong national pride and sensitivity:

. . . they are given both to undue chauvinism for national achievements and to painful embarrassment at what they conceive to be national shortcomings. More positively, they are genuinely concerned with the interests of their whole society, placing that before family interests or the advantage of provinces or classes. (Webb, 1957)

This has several implications for the aged. One is the strong sense of duty to the nation which motivates many of the aged to keep working (Chapter 5) and to be useful around the house and in the community (Chapter 4). On the other hand, since the aged are recognized as an important part of the nation, many Japanese, particularly Japanese officials, seem to consider it a matter of national honor to improve the conditions of the aged. They are very sensitive, for example, to comparative statistics which show that the Japanese aged have lower levels of social security benefits and a relatively small number of institutions for care of the aged.

Concern with politeness and deference toward superiors and "saving face" is another traditional characteristic of Japanese. Many Americans, whose social usages prescribe more informality, frankness, and directness, have criticized this concern as evasive, hypocritical, and dishonest. It may be that Japanese tend to be more evasive in some situations, but this is usually motivated by a desire to avoid the rudeness of contradiction, criticism, or outright refusal. "Polite lies" are used throughout the civilized world to avoid such rudeness and embarrassment. The Japanese probably differ only in the degree to which they resort to such tactics. As for dishonesty, the Japanese are probably more generally honest in the legal sense that Westerners. Most Japanese have a deep respect for the law and personal property. This can be illustrated in many ways: it is still relatively safe for women to walk the streets at night alone (Tokyo has been called the "last safe city in the world"); bicycles are often left unlocked in public places and are considered completely safe if locked with a flimsy lock which would be practically no deterrent in much of the United States; most items left on trains or subways are turned in to the lost and found department; despite the flimsy construction of most Japanese doors and windows there are relatively few house burglaries.

The politeness and deference shown toward the "honorable elders" may be criticized as empty ritual on the grounds that modern Japanese do not really respect the aged as much as the forms of respect would indicate. This becomes a moot point on which conclusive evidence is lacking. (See Chapter 7.) In a sense, much of this book is about how the Japanese express their respect for the aged through maintaining their integration in the society.

Many observers have pointed out a dominant aesthetic sense in the Japanese temperament:

Universal appreciation and preservation of the natural beauty of their homeland and a love of aesthetically pleasing pastimes (flower viewing, flower arranging, the tea ceremony, for instance) are striking instances of this. In addition, they maintain traditions of fine style in the manufacture of everyday utilitarian objects. (Webb, 1957)

I was often impressed with this aesthetic appreciation in Japan. For example, I often saw flower arrangements, potted plants, and goldfish tanks in places where they would not appear in my Western world: on train turnstiles, in police stations, and even public toilets. This aesthetic appreciation seems to be particularly cultivated by older Japanese. The arts of *bonsai* (growing miniature trees), flower arranging, tea ceremony, gardening, folk dancing, chanting of *yokyoku* (texts of the classical dramas) and other poetry, writing of *haiku,* and calligraphy, all are frequently reported hobbies of the older Japanese. All these activities usually are highly valued because they contribute to the creation and preservation of beauty.

Another traditional Japanese trait is a more casual and flexible attitude toward time and scheduling. It has been said that "the Japanese are not tyrannized by the clock, nor is there an emphasis on scheduling of activities" (Smith, 1961, p. 99). It is claimed that this makes older people more accepting of the approaching end of time for them and of their increased leisure.

The older adult is not, then, a prisoner of time, nor does he feel that it is running out for him. He makes no effort to appear younger than he is. The minutes, hours, and days simply pass, filled up with a variety of activities which are performed as the need to do them arises. Time does not drag and it does not threaten; it is there to be used but it does not stretch emptily before the older person (Smith, 1961, pp. 99f).

Finally, there are two social characteristics of Japan which make transportation for the aged less of a problem than in most of the United States. The first is that, although the big cities now have big department stores, most daily shopping takes place in small neighborhood grocery stores and specialty shops. Most neighborhoods have their own meat store, fish shop, vegetable and fruit store, canned and dry-goods store, as well as several other small shops specializing in shoes, flowers, electric appliances, hardware, pottery and utensils, etc. Thus, most aged are within walking distance of shops that can supply most of their daily needs. These small, family-owned and operated shops also provide considerable employment for the aged (Chapter 5).

The other fact is that the public transit system in Japan is one of the most elaborate and convenient in the world. For example, one can commute to downtown Tokyo from most of the suburbs in about a half-hour on the express trains. Similarly, one can get from any part of the central city of Tokyo to any other part in about a half-hour on the subways. Thus, the need for private automobiles to provide transportation is much less in Japan than in most of the United States. Since many of the aged cannot afford an automobile or may have trouble driving, these simple ecological facts probably make a significant contribution to the better integration of the aged in Japanese society.

THE TRADITION OF RESPECT FOR THE AGED

The following chapters present and discuss the modern manifestations of respect for the aged. Here we wish only to sketch the traditional background. There seem to be two main roots: the vertical society and the filial piety. The vertical society establishes the right of all aged to general respect from younger persons; filial piety specifies the obligations owed to one's own parents and grandparents.

The theory of Japan's vertical society has been most clearly elaborated by Nakane and most of the following description has been drawn from her recent book (1972). Put in its simplest form, this theory states that most Japanese interpersonal relationships are determined by a delicately graded hierarchy or system of vertical relationships. Vertical relationships are those between superior and inferior, such as parent and child, master and servant, teacher and student, senior and junior persons. These are contrasted with horizontal relationships which are those between equals, such as between colleagues and friends in our society. It is part of the theory that, in Japanese society, even relationships between colleagues and friends become vertical depending on age, sex, and other factors.

Because of the overwhelming ascendancy of this vertical orientation, even a set of individuals sharing identical qualifications tend to create a *difference* among themselves. As this is reinforced, an amazingly delicate and intricate system of *ranking* takes shape.

There are numerous examples of this ranking process. Among lathe operators with the same qualifications there exist differences of rank based on relative age, year of entry into the company or length of continuous service; among professors at the same college, rank can be assessed by the formal date of appointment; among commissioned officers in the former Japanese army the differences between ranks were very great, and it is said that even among second lieutenants distinct ranking was made on the basis of order of appointment (Nakane, 1972, pp. 25).

As is obvious from these examples, age and seniority are among the most important criteria for these vertical rankings. It is true that age may be superseded by other bases of status. For example, the head of a household, regardless of age, occupies the "highest" seat in the household and his retired father retreats to a "lower" seat. Nevertheless, there is a residual respect which most older persons traditionally retain in relations with most younger persons. The many forms of deference behavior in both public and private life which show this respect will be described in Chapter 7. It is sufficient to recognize here that seniority is a primary basis for the vertical society in Japan and that this social structure tends to maintain the relatively high status of older Japanese.

The other root of this traditional respect is filial piety which, in turn, goes back to both Confucian precepts and the even more ancient ancestor worship. Hearn describes ancestor worship as the "real religion of Japan:"

> The real religion of Japan, the religion still professed in one form or other, by the entire nation (1900), is that cult which has been the foundation of all civilized religion, and of all civilized society—Ancestor-worship. In the course of thousands of years this original cult has undergone modifications, and has assumed various shapes; but everywhere in Japan its fundamental character remains unchanged. Without including the different Buddhist forms of ancestor-worship, we find three distinct rites of purely Japanese origin, subsequently modified to some degree by Chinese influence and ceremonial. These Japanese forms of the cult are all classed together under the name of "Shinto," which signifies, "The Way of the Gods." . . . The three forms of the Shinto worship of ancestors are the Domestic Cult, the Communal Cult, and the State Cult;—or, in other words, the worship of family ancestors, the worship of clan or tribal ancestors, and the worship of imperial ancestors (Hearn, 1955, pp. 21f).

One can question whether ancestor worship was the foundation of all civilized religion, but it seems certain that it was the foundation of Japanese religions. To appreciate the supreme importance of ancestor worship in ancient Japan, one need only consider the implications of the five basic beliefs of this religion:

I. The dead remain in this world,—haunting their tombs, and also their former homes, and sharing invisibly in the life of their living descendants;

II. All the dead become gods, in the sense of acquiring supernatural power; but they retain the characters which distinguish them during life;

III. The happiness of the dead depends upon the respectful service rendered them by the living; and the happiness of the living depends upon the fulfilment of pious duty to the dead; . . .

IV. Every event in the world, good or evil,—fair seasons or plentiful harvests,—flood and famine,—tempest and tidal-wave and earthquake,—is the work of the dead;

V. All human actions, good or bad, are controlled by the dead (Hearn, 1955, pp. 31).

Hearn probably exaggerated the actual beliefs in the power of the ancestral ghosts, but it was generally considered important that the ghosts be kept happy through reverence and nourishment:

But, in spite of their supernatural power, the dead are still dependent upon the living for happiness. Though viewless, save in dreams, they need earthly nourishment and homage,—food and drink, and the reverence of their descendants. Each ghost must rely for such comfort upon its living kindred;—only through the devotion of that kindred can it ever find repose. Each ghost must have shelter,—a fitting tomb;—each must have offerings. While honorably sheltered and properly nourished the spirit is pleased, and will aid in maintaining the good-fortune of its propitiators. But if refused the sepulchral home, the funeral rites, the offerings of food and fire and drink, the spirit will suffer from hunger and cold and thirst, and, becoming angered, will act malevolently and contrive misfortune for those by whom it has been neglected (Hearn, 1955, pp. 29).

It is but a small step from this ancestor worship to filial piety toward living parents and grandparents. Since reverence and devotion to dead ancestors are of supreme importance, respect and duty toward living parents and grandparents (who will soon become dead ancestors) become the second most important thing in life.

Oyakòko, or obligation to parents, was one of two unconditional and absolute duties (the other being *chu*, obligation to the Emperor, the law, and Japan). These two duties were so absolute and unconditional that there was a special word for them, *gimu*, to distinguish them from all lesser duties. *Gimu* were such unlimited obligations that it was said, "One never repays one ten-thousandth of *gimu*" (Benedict, 1946). It is hard for a Westerner to understand the unconditional nature of this filial piety:

. . . filial piety became in Japan a duty one had to fulfill even if it meant condoning a parent's vice and injustice. It could be abrogated only if it came into conflict with one's obligation to the Emperor, but certainly not when one's parent was unworthy or when he was destroying one's happiness.

In one of their modern movies a mother comes upon some money her married son, a village schoolmaster, has collected from the villagers to redeem a young schoolgirl about to be sold by her parents to a house of prostitution because they are starving in a rural famine. The schoolmaster's mother steals the money from her son although she is not poor; she runs a respectable restaurant of her own. Her son knows that she has taken it but he had to shoulder the blame himself. His wife discovers the truth, leaves a suicide note taking all responsibility for the loss of the money, and drowns herself and their baby. Publicity follows but the mother's part in the tragedy is not even called in question. The son has fulfilled the law of filial piety and goes off alone to Nokkaido to build his character so that he can strengthen himself for like tests in coming years. He is a virtuous hero (Benedict, 1946, pp. 119).

In this respect, Japanese filial piety goes beyond even the Chinese Confucian precepts. In the Chinese ethic, a parent must be benevolent toward his children in order to claim their devotion. In traditional Japan, one should per-

form his filial piety regardless of how tyrannical or dis-
agreeable his parents are. Indeed, in ancient Japan "the
patriarch of the Japanese family appears to have had . . .
powers of life and death over all the members of the household . . . . The family was a despotism" (Hearn, 1955, pp.
71).

A classic example of filial piety is the supposedly true
story of Taiko Hideyoshi, a famous Japanese ruler during
the sixteenth century. When he was nearing sixty he lost
both his one little son, whom he loved dearly, and his
younger brother. In order to forget his sorrows:

> . . . he determined to do something extraordinary which should make
> a noise in the world. He planneed a vast expedition against the neigh-
> boring country of Korea, and constructed many strong fighting ships
> and ordered his array.
>
> But the mother of Hideyoshi, who was then much over eighty years
> of age, was so disturbed in mind at hearing of her son's great scheme
> that she fell sick. Then the mighty warrior, most filial of sons, gave up
> his hope to lead this expedition in person and set his headquarters in
> Nagoya, whence to overlook affairs (Harris, 1937).

Thus, filial piety may require even great rulers to change
their conduct of national and international affairs in order
to defer to the wishes of parents.

Much of this tradition is being questioned and rejected
by the younger generations in modern Japan, but it should
be clear by now that respect for the aged has strong roots
growing out of both Japan's basic social structure and her
fundamental religious beliefs.

SUMMARY

Japan's climate is similar to that of the United States;
most of it is somewhat warmer than that of Great Britain
and Denmark. Japan is much more densely populated than

the United States but not much more so than Great Britain.
Japan is clearly one of the most industrialized nations in
the world with a higher proportion of her gross national
product from manufacturing than the United States, Great
Britain, or Denmark. Her total gross national product is
second only to the United States; her per capita income,
however, is lower than the three comparison countries.
She has a higher rate of natural increase and a lower percentage aged 65 and over than the comparison countries,
but recent decreases in birth and death rates are expected
to rapidly increase the percentage aged 65 and over.

The Japanese are relatively homogeneous racially and
ethnically which may facilitate the integration of the aged.
Some social-psychological traits relevant to this analysis
are: strong national pride, concern with politeness and deference toward superiors, a dominant aesthetic sense, and
a more casual attitude toward time. Transportation is less
of a problem for the aged in Japan because of the many
neighborhood shops and the elaborate system of public
transportation.

The tradition of respect for the aged has strong roots
both in the vertical social system and in the unconditional duty of filial piety which derives from the fundamental Japanese religion, ancestor worship. Thus, the
ecology and economic system of Japan are similiar to that
of western industrialized nations, but her social system
and culture have distinctive elements which have helped
maintain the relatively high status and integration of older
Japanese.

3
Health and
Medical Care

Before the fox-shrine[1]
make one wish: fame, fortune, love?
No, I pray for health.

We begin our analysis with health and medical care because it appears that these are the most frequent concerns
of the aged, both in Japan and the rest of the world (Cantril, 1965). Studies at the Duke Center for the Study of
Aging and Human Development found health to be the
one factor most closely related to life satisfaction (Palmore
and Luikart, 1972). A survey of Japanese over 60 years of
age, in which they were asked to choose the two most important things for future life satisfaction, found that 76 percent chose health as the first most important thing (Office
of the Prime Minister, 1973). This proportion remained
close to 75 percent regardless of sex, age, density, education, employment, or present health! Thus, it appears to
be the primary concern for all types of older Japanese.

Health is also related to the two theories we shall be
testing. Health probably affects the status and integration
of the aged, and it clearly affects the amount of activity in
which they can engage.

[1]A fox-shrine (*Inarisan*) is a local shrine to the god of harvests, before which it
is customary to throw a coin in a box, clap your hands, or ring a bell to call the
attention of the gods, and then pray for something.

CROSS-CULTURAL COMPARISONS

To measure overall health, however, is a difficult problem, regardless of whether survey-interviewer techniques
or medical examinations are used. This becomes doubly
difficult when cross-cultural comparisons are made because of differences in conceptions of health and illness between cultures. However, there is an indirect measure of a
population's health which permits accurate cross-cultural
comparison: life expectancy. A comparison of Japanese
life expectancy, both at birth and at age 65, with that of
three other industrialized countries shows that Japan was
slightly behind in 1960, but was about equal to the other
three countries by 1970 (Table 3-1). (There was little or no
change in the life expectancies in the other countries between 1960 and 1970.) Thus, this measure indicates that the
health of the Japanese aged is about the same as that of the
aged in other industrialized countries.

Another indirect measure of health among the aged
that is fairly comparable between countries is mobility

Table 3-1. Life expectancy in Japan is similar to other industrialized
countries (years of age)

	Japan 1970	Japan 1960	U. S. 1960	Britain 1960	Denmark 1960
At birth					
Men	69.3	65.3	67.0	68.1	70.4
Women	74.7	70.2	73.6	74.0	73.8
At age 65					
Men	12.5	12.0	13.0	12.0	13.8
Women	15.5	15.0	16.1	15.2	15.1

Source for Japanese life expectancy: *Welfare Journal,* p. 5 and Ministry of Health and Welfare, 1972, p. 10.

status: that is, whether a person is institutionalized, bed-fast, or housebound. One difficulty with this indicator is that it is concerned only with the sickest or most disabled segment (20 percent or less) of the aged population. It does not tell us anything about the health of the other 80 percent or more. However, a comparison of the mobility status of the aged in Japan with that of the other three industrialized societies shows that although few of the Japanese are in-stitutionalized, there are substantially more Japanese re-ported to be bedfast or housebound (Table 3-2). If one adds together the institutionalized and the bedfast, on the as-sumption that both categories show similar severe limita-tions, then the total for these two categories is somewhat lower in Japan then in the other countries. But many more of the older Japanese are reported as "housebound." There may be several explanations for this. There may be some cultural difference in the willingness to admit or re-port that a person is housebound. Shanas suggests, for example, that "Old people in the United States, more than old people in Europe, seem to feel that to admit illness or incapacity is somehow psychologically wrong" (1968, p. 46). Thus we cannot be sure whether there really are

Table 3-2. Japanese are less institutionalized but more often bedfast or housebound (percentage distribution)

Aged over 65 Who Are:	Japan	U. S.	Britain	Denmark
Institutionalized	1	4	4	5
Bedfast	4	2	3	2
Housebound	16	6	11	8

Source: Japan-institutionalized from *Welfare Journal*, p. 19; % bedfast from Ministry of Health and Welfare, 1972, p. 3; % housebound from Office of the Prime Minister, 1973, p. 78; other countries—Shanas and Associates, 1968.

more housebound among older Japanese, or just more willing to report being housebound. An explanation advanced by some Japanese gerontologists is that the aged in Japan are allowed and even encouraged to become housebound and dependent more than elsewhere; that other cultures put more emphasis on the advantages of maintaining independence by going out of the house. A third explanation is that the term used in the survey for "housebound" literally means "sometimes in bed and sometimes out." It does not specifically mean that a person never goes out of the house. Therefore, there may be some included who are not entirely housebound. In the light of all these explanations, it seems probable that the higher percentage of Japanese reported housebound does not mean that the aged in Japan have poorer health than in other countries.

Suicide rates are an international statistic which might be considered as an indicator of mental illness. Japanese women over 65 had the fourth highest rate in 1966-67 (Metropolitan Life, 1972). Furthermore, suicide rates in Japan increase in old age more than in the United States, especially among women (Figure 3-1). However, these statistics do not indicate, in our opinion, any more mental illness, or even more unhappiness, among Japan's aged. It probably is simply a result of the ancient Japanese tradition of using suicide to preserve the family honor, or save face, or take revenge on someone, or terminate one's misery, or "solve" a host of other problems. Japanese literature and real life both demonstrate this greater tendency of the traditional Japanese culture to approve or at least tolerate suicide more than other cultures. The higher suicide rates among older Japanese, compared to younger Japanese, probably show that there are a few more aged with extreme loneliness, severe illness, poverty, and other

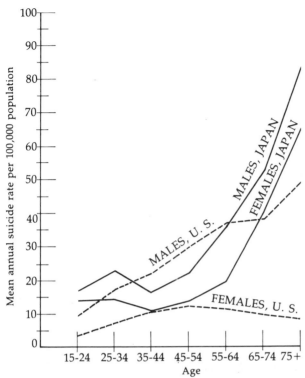

Figure 3-1. *Suicide rates for United States and Japan, 1963-66*
Source: World Health Organization, 1968.

miseries which may lead to suicide. Despite the higher rate, suicides are less than one percent of all deaths among older Japanese. Also, there has been a marked decline in Japanese suicide rates at all ages since 1956-57, which probably indicates a decline in the tradition of suicide described above (Metropolitan Life, 1972).

FACTORS RELATED TO HEALTH

Subjective health ratings, such as "good, fair, or poor

health," are almost impossible to compare cross-culturally because of cultural differences in the meanings of words like "good health." However, within the Japanese culture we can examine the factors related to these subjective ratings and make some inferences about these factors and overall health in Japan.

Cross-tabulations of subjective health rating by age show the expected negative relationship to increasing age (Table 3-3). This shows that in Japan, as elsewhere, a growing minority of the aged suffer from poor health as they grow older. But the impressive thing about his cross-tabulation is that even at age 70 and over, a majority (57 percent) report good or ordinary health. This and the previous table show how wrong is the usual stereotype that most persons over 70 are in poor health or are disabled. Why does this stereotype persist despite clear evidence to the contrary (Palmore, 1969)? Shanas and associates suggest two reasons: "We only notice old people when they are ill and enfeebled" and, until recently, most of the studies of aging have been done on the sick and institutionalized (1968, pp. 18).

The second part of Table 3-3 shows that the men admit poor health less often than women. This seems to be a universal tendency at all age levels in all modern societies studied. Yet, since women at each age level have less mortality than men, it seems unlikely that women are actually sicker than men. The most probable explanation is that in male-dominated societies men are expected to be stronger and more robust than women, and therefore men resist admitting illness more than women.

Are cities with their pollution and crowding detrimental to the health of the aged? The cross-tabulation of health and density of population fails to show any clear

Table 3-3. Health of older Japanese (percentage distribution)

	Good	Ordinary	Poor	Total
Total aged:				
50+	35	39	25	100
50-59	40	44	16	100
60-69	36	38	26	100
70+	26	31	42	100
Men 60+	36	35	28	100
Women 60+	27	36	35	100
Area:				
Tokyo	41	38	21	100
9 large cities	26	50	24	100
Other cities over 100,000	38	36	25	100
Cities under 100,000	37	38	24	100
Rural	34	39	26	100

Source: Office of the Prime Minister, 1973.

evidence for this theory (Table 3-3). There is little difference between various size cities and the rural areas in the
proportion reporting poor health, except that Tokyo has
fewer reporting poor health and more reporting good
health. It seems unlikely that Tokyo is really a more healthy
environment for the aged than less dense areas. Perhaps
there is a selective factor operating so that fewer of the un-
healthy aged emigrate to or stay in Tokyo.

MEDICAL CARE

Obtaining and paying for adequate medical care is a
major problem for many older Americans (Palmore,
1972b). Despite the coverage of most older Americans by
Medicare, this program in fact covers less than half the
actual medical costs of the aged. In contrast, most older
Japanese can now get free, or at little cost, most of their

medical care. Since the beginning of 1973 most Japanese over age 70 (more than half of the total over 65) get all medical care (including physician-prescribed medicines) completely free. There are some income restrictions so that wealthy aged do not get this free care. Some cities, such as Tokyo, extend this free medical care down to age 65. The younger aged not covered by this free medical care program are covered by one of the other medical insurance programs. Under the Employees' Health Insurance programs, sick employees receive free (or for token payments) all medical and dental care including office and home visits, drugs, therapy, prosthetics, surgery, hospitalization, out-patient care, nursing, and transportation, and for a practically unlimited duration. Dependents of the employee, however, must pay 30 percent of the cost of service. Under the National Health Insurance program, which covers everybody else, the extent of the medical care is the same, and the program pays 70 percent of the cost. However, "Reductions, exemptions, and other variations in the [30 percent] patient's share are allowed for persons who find difficulty in paying their share" (Ministry of Health and Welfare, 1972, pp. 49). Thus, the financial barriers to medical care in Japan are much less formidable than in the United States.

But there is always the barrier of the time and effort required to get even free medical care. How many of the sick older Japanese acutally get medical care? The most recent survey found that 85 percent of those over 60 who said they were in poor health also reported that they got medical care regularly (Office of the Prime Minister, 1973). This appears to be a high percentage, considering that many of those in poor health have conditions which do not benefit from medical treatment.

Another special provision for the health of the aged is the program of free annual health examinations for all persons over 65. These are comprehensive screening examinations followed up by more detailed diagnosis and individual counseling when needed. Although these are available to all the aged, only about one-fifth actually get them. Presumably, most of the remainder either had another recent examination or believed they were in such good health that they did not need an examination.

What do the aged in good health do to maintain their health? A fourth reported that they are careful to eat a good diet, about a fifth of the men reported that they engaged in sports or exercise (but only one-tenth of the women reported this), and about a fourth reported each of the following: keep a regular schedule, avoid overexertion, work at a job that is not too difficult (Table 3-4). Less than a tenth reported getting medical examinations, medical care, and taking medicines.

As an illustration of the importance given to exercise in maintaining good health among the aged, there is a widespread practice of starting off each day in homes for the

Table 3-4. What healthy Japanese aged do to keep healthy (percentage distribution)

	Men 60 +	Women 60 +
Careful diet	26	26
Sports or exercise	22	10
Regular schedule	24	19
Avoid over-exertion	21	25
Have a job that is not too difficult	20	16
Medical examinations and care	10	5
Medicine	6	9

Source: Office of the Prime Minister, 1973. (Totals add to more than 100 percent because of multiple answers.)

aged with a combination group exercise and folkdance. I was always impressed as I passed the home for the aged on the way to the office to see about 100 feeble residents on the lawn in front doing setting-up exercises in time to music or going through the steps and gestures of a graceful Japanese folkdance.

SUMMARY

Three-fourths of all types of Japanese aged chose health as the most important thing for future satisfaction. Life expectancy and the proportion institutionalized or bed-fast indicated that the health of older Japanese is similar to that of the aged in other industrialized countries. Higher proportions reported as housebound and higher suicide rates were discounted as being primarily due to cultural differences rather than differences in health. Subjective reports of poor health increased with age, but even over age 70 a majority reported ordinary or good health. There seemed to be no clear relationship between population density and health.

Most older Japanese can get free, or at little cost, most medical care. The most frequently reported ways of maintaining health were eating a good diet, engaging in sports or exercise, keeping a regular schedule, avoiding over-exertion, and working at a job that is not too difficult.

4
The Family
and Living
Arrangements

When hair is snow-white
what can warm the heart? Only
family and friends.

Next to health, older Japanese consider family relationships to be the most important thing for life satisfaction.
The survey in which older Japanese were asked what are
the two most important things for future life satisfaction,
found that the second choice was most often: "Family respect and care" (Office of the Prime Minister, 1973).

The basic fact which underlies typical family relations
of older Japanese and which makes these relations markedly different from those of most other industrialized countries is the fact that over three-fourths of Japanese aged 65
or more *live with their children* (Office of the Prime Minister, 1973). This is true of all areas except Tokyo, where 68%
live with their children, and true in all age groups (Table
4-1). This is in contrast with only 25 percent in the United
States, 33 percent in Britain, and 15 percent in Denmark
(Shanas and associates, 1968). Furthermore, the typical
household of the older Japanese contains not only his or
her son, but grandchildren as well. For example, even in
Tokyo over half of those over 60 live with children *and*

Table 4-1. Three-fourths of older Japanese live with their children

Age Groups	% Live with Child			% Not Live with Child	
	Total	Married Child	Unmarried Child	Total	Have No Child
Total 50+	76	44	32	24	6
Tokyo	68	37	30	32	8
9 Other Large Cities	74	31	44	26	8
Other Cities 100,000+	75	39	37	25	6
Less Than 100,000	76	46	30	24	5
Rural	80	55	24	20	5
Age:					
50-59	77	27	50	23	5
60-69	75	57	18	25	6
70+	77	69	8	23	6

Source: Office of the Prime Minister, 1973.

grandchildren (Tokyo Metropolitan Government, 1971). In contrast, Stehouwer states: "The three-generation household represents a structure which is rare in almost all industrial societies" (Shanas and associates, 1968, p. 184). Clearly, Japan is an important exception to such a generalization.

Even more of the single* older Japanese (compared to couples) live with their children (83 percent: Table 4-2). Of those single aged persons who do not live with their children, a third live with relatives and a few more live with non-relatives, so that only 9 percent of single aged live alone. Thus, it is rare to find an older Japanese living by himself (only 5 percent of the total aged), while in the comparison industrialized countries about half the single aged live by themselves.

However, many people discount this high proportion

*"Single" includes all persons without a spouse present.

living with their children by assuming that the proportion is rapidly declinging, that the majority of younger couples want to live separately from their parents, and that only economic necessity forces them to live with their aging parents. For example, a feature article in *The New York Times* on the aged in Japan stated, "Although about 80 percent of the elderly still live with their children, that figure is rapidly decreasing. Young married adults in the cities prefer to live by themselves with their own children" (Halloran, 1972). Each of these assumptions is demonstrably false.

In 1953 the proportion of Japanese over 60 living with their children was 81 percent (National Life Center, 1972) and in 1973 this proportion declined to 75 percent (Prime Minister's Office, 1973). This is a decline of only 3 percent

Table 4-2. Composition of households of 65+ in four countries (percentage distribution)

Composition	Japan		Britain		U. S.		Denmark	
	M	F	M	F	M	F	M	F
Couples:								
Alone	16	15	67	68	77	82	80	84
With Child	79	79	29	28	18	15	17	14
With Relatives	4	5	3	5	3	2	1	—
Non-Relatives	1	1	1	2	2	1	2	2
Total	100	100	100	100	100	100	100	100
Single:								
Alone	10	8	37	45	52	46	58	63
With Child	82	84	41	37	38	37	20	21
With Relatives	6	6	14	13	11	22	6	7
Non-Relatives	2	2	8	5	8	5	10	9
Total	100	100	100	100	100	100	100	100

Source: Japan—Nasu, 1973; other countries—Shanas, 1968.

per decade. At that rate, over two-thirds of the aged will still be living with their children in the year 2000.

As for preference in living arrangements, a majority of parents at all age levels and in both cities and rural areas favor joint households and wish to live with their children when they retire (Table 4-3). The only exception is among college graduates who have a majority wishing to live separately from their children. It is true that more of the younger than older parents and more in the urban than rural areas wish to live separately from their children which suggests a continuation of the present slow rate of decline in percent of aged living with their children.

Table 4-3. The majority of Japanese parents favor joint households with children

	% Wishing to Live with Children	% Wishing to Live Separately
Total	60	40
Age:		
20-29	52	48
30-39	56	44
40-49	60	40
60+	74	26
Area:		
Tokyo	50	50
6 Large Cities	53	47
Other Cities of 100,000+	55	45
Cities Less Than 100,000	63	37
Rural	69	31
Parents' Education:		
Elementary School	79	21
Junior High School	66	34
High School	51	49
College	43	57

Source: National Life Center, 1972. ("Don't know" and no answer categories excluded.)

As for the assumption that most joint households are caused by economic necessity, the evidence is again to the contrary. I could find no national data on the attitudes of younger persons toward living with their parents, but one survey in the Tokyo metropolitan area found that most housewives in apartments (aged 30-59) who lived with parents favored a continuation of living in joint households. Only 3 percent wanted to live separately (Japan Housing Foundation, 1973). In a survey of parents over age 50, those who said they wanted to live with their children upon retirement were asked whether they would want to live together or separately if they had sufficient money and personal care to live in separate homes. Ninety-one percent of those responding said they would still prefer to live together with their children (Office ot the Prime Minister, 1973). The same survey also found that 95 percent of those actually living with their children wanted to continue living with their children, and a third of those living separately would rather live with their children. Finally, only 20 percent gave "financial aid" as a reason for wanting to live with their children, while the rest gave reasons such as: "It is natural to live with your children"; "Companionship with children"; and "Get care from children" (Table 4-4). There probably is some bias in these answers toward the socially expected type, but it appears that the joint household is not only the typical living arrangement, but is usually preferred for reasons other than economic necessity.

It is also significant that of those who said they wanted to live separately, most still wanted to live within the same compound or at least within walking distance of their children, and only one third wanted to live beyond walking distance of their children.

Table 4-4. Few Japanese aged want to live with children because of financial aid

Reasons for Wanting to Live with Children	% Giving Reason
Get care from children	38
It is natural to live with children	31
Companionship with children	30
Financial aid from children	20
Enjoyment of caring for children and grandchildren	9
Convenience	8
Children want me to live with them	6
Other reasons	2

Source: National Life Center, 1972. (Percentages add up to more than 100 because some gave multiple reasons.)

This basic difference in living arrangements between Japan and the comparison industrialized countries cannot be explained by differences in demographic characteristics such as marital status or having surviving children. The proportion of older Japanese with a spouse present is similar to those of the other countries, although somewhat fewer of the Japanese women have a spouse (Table 4-5). There are 14 to 20 percent more of the aged in Japan with surviving children (which is probably due to a higher mar-

Table 4-5. Marital status and children of those 65+ in four countries (percentage distribution)

	Japan	U. S.	Britain	Denmark
Men:				
With spouse	76	76	70	70
With surviving child	94	83	80	84
Women:				
With spouse	31	38	34	42
With surviving child	94	82	74	81

Source: *Welfare Journal*, 1971 and Office of the Prime Minister, 1973.

riage rate—99 percent have married—and to the practice of childless couples adopting children), but this would account for only a small part of the differences between Japan and the comparison countries in proportions living with children.

Two other differences in the pattern of joint households between Japan and the comparison countries are worth noting. While the joint households in the comparison countries tend to consist of an older person or couple with an unmarried child ("nuclear" families), three-fourths of the joint households in Japan are with married children ("stem" families) (Ministry of Health and Welfare, 1970). Indeed, in the United States and Denmark less than two percent of aged couples live with married children. This shows that joint households in the comparison countries tend to be confined to those few cases in which either the child or the parent is spouseless, whereas in Japan joint households are the dominant pattern for married and unmarried parents and children alike.

The other difference is that in the comparison countries joint households tend to be with the daughter, while in Japan the opposite is true: there are four times as many joint households with the son's family as with the daughter's (National Life Center, 1972). This indicates that in Japan the parent-son tie is stronger because of the tradition of filial responsibility in which it is the son's responsibility to care for his parents, while the daughter tends to cut her ties with her own parents upon marriage and transfers her loyalties to her husband's family and parents. This tradition of parents living with the son's family often creates the well-known mother-in-law versus daughter-in-law conflicts.

Another note on joint households in Japan: the typical

pattern is for the parents to live continuously with their child (usually the oldest son), rather than to live separately during middle age and move back in with the child during their last years. In Tokyo, for example, three-fourths of the aged had lived continuously with one or more children and only 8 percent had moved back in with a child after living separately (Nasu, 1973). Furthermore, those who lived continuously with their children had much less despondency than those who were living alone. This seems to indicate that in Japan joint households promote life satisfaction for the aged.

Finally, how crowded are these joint households? Three-fourths of all Japanese over age 60 have at least their own bedroom (*Welfare Journal*, 1971). This proportion drops to about two-thirds in households with over four members (joint households). This seems to indicate that there is little more crowding in the joint households than in separate households.

Many of the older Japanese who are listed as sharing a joint household actually live in a separate part of the house or apartment, with some separate cooking facilities and may eat some of their meals separately from the rest of the family. Especially in rural Japan, it is sometimes the custom for the older parents to retire to a separate little house behind the main house. These practices of semi-separate facilities within a joint household probably reduce tensions that might otherwise develop.

FUNCTIONS IN THE JOINT HOUSEHOLD

Why do so many of the older Japanese live with their children? We have discussed the tradition of filial responsibility and the general reasons given in surveys

(Table 4-4), but these reasons do not sufficiently recognize the important functions that most aged perform in their joint households. For example, there is the function of the *rusuban*, or caretaker (literally "watcher during absences"). Because most Japanese houses have sliding doors and are generally less burglar-proof than Western houses, it is usually considered necessary to have someone stay in the house most of the time as a caretaker to prevent burglary. This is an easy function for the aged, and one which most aged in joint households appear to perform frequently.

The grandmother appears to perform more important functions than the grandfather. Typically, she prepares or supervises preparation of meals, supervises younger children, does small gardening, and helps with the laundry.

. . .During the busy season everyone capable of active labour is indispensable. The grandmother, on the other hand, stays at home doing the housework or tending the babies, and sometimes acts as a liason officer to the family (Koyama, 1961, pp. 93).

In addition, grandmother is usually the perpetuator of religious affairs. It is she who makes offerings to the god of the kitchen and others, and visits the shrines, making pilgrimage during the ceremonial days. Especially in rural areas, the grandmother often cares for the children to free the mothers for field work.

Criticism has often been directed at the fact that the grandmothers and not the mothers of the schoolchildren are present at the meetings of the Parent-Teacher Association (PTA) in rural communities. From the standpoint of the farm families, the attendance of the grandmothers is taken for granted because the mothers are needed in the fields for doing the farm work (Koyama, 1961, pp. 93).

In urban areas also, the grandparents free the mother for outside work by caring for the children.

Grandfathers appear to be somewhat less active, although there is considerable variability in this regard.

(The retired grandfather) position is assumed gradually and has some variability. Retirement from a full work load and full authority to a routine of light tasks and advisor functions marks the step-by-step assumption of the role . . . . Skilled handicrafts, menial tasks, and some baby-tending become his main economic functions (Silberman, 1962, pp. 145).

An especially important function of both grandmothers and grandfathers is that of affectional support for the grandchildren. Grandparents appear to have less important functions than parents in the areas of task performance, discipline, and problem solving, but in the area of comfort and affectional support the grandparents are usually most important. In many cases, one child may be assigned to the grandmother and another to the grandfather. They bathe and sleep together and help each other (Vogel, 1967, pp. 224).

A survey of persons over 60 living with their children found help in the family business was the most frequent main role in the household for men, with gardening being second (Table 4-6). Over a third of the women specified

Table 4-6. Housework and help in family business are the most frequent main roles in the household (percentage distribution of Japanese over 60 living with children)

Main Role	Total	Men	Women
Housework	26	14	36
Help in family business	21	27	16
Gardening	14	19	10
Care of grandchild	11	7	14
Other role	17	20	14
No special role	11	12	10
Total	100	100	100

Source: Ministry of Health and Welfare, 1972b.

housework as their main role, with help in family business and care of grandchildren running a close second and third place. Only eleven percent said they had no special role in the household. Another survey found that in a majority of households with a woman aged 60-69, the older woman had *primary* responsibility for housekeeping (National Life Center, 1972).

One of the most important functions of Japanese elders is that of senior advisor on family problems. Over two-thirds of Japanese over 60 report that they are consulted on family problems, and this proportion is even higher among the men and among the employed (Table 4-7). In earlier times the decision of the elder on all matters was final and usually accepted by all family members. These days the authority of the elders appears to be quite variable, depending on which matter is in question (the elders have more authority in "traditional" matters and less in regard to "modern" matters such as those involving technology), how much power and competence the elder retains, etc. Nevertheless, most elders are at least consulted on some family problems.

In the light of all these functions, it is understandable

Table 4-7. Over two-thirds of older Japanese are consulted by their children on family problems (percentage distribution of Japanese over 60)

	Total	Men	Women	Employed	Not Employed
Consulted	67	73	62	80	57
Not consulted	32	26	37	18	42
No answer	1	1	1	2	1
Total	100	100	100	100	100

Source: Ministry of Health and Welfare, 1972b.

why most of the normal aged living with their children
are considered valuable members of the household rather
than merely financial burdens.

SEPARATE HOUSEHOLDS

What of the older Japanese living in separate households? How much are they integrated into the family? One
measure is the proximity of the nearest child's household.
Presumably, those who live closer generally see more of
their families than those who live farther away. The majority of those in separate households live within 30
minutes' travel of their nearest child (Table 4-8). This is
also true of the comparison three industrialized countries.
In Japan, only 7 percent of the total aged parents (including both separate and joint households) live more than a
half hour away from children. In the other countries about
a quarter live more than a half hour away. It is therefore at
least possible for most aged in all countries to see their children on an almost daily basis.

Indeed, 85 percent of the older Japanese parents did see
their children on a daily or almost daily basis, largely be-

Table 4-8. Proximity of children to aged parents in four countries
(percentage distribution)

Proximity	Japan	U. S.	Britain	Denmark
Same household	80	28	42	20
Within 10 min.	7	33	24	32
11-30 min.	5	16	16	23
More than 30 min.	7	23	18	25
Total	100	100	100	100

Source: Japan—*Welfare Journal,* 1971; other countries—Shanas and
associates, 1968. (Aged without children omitted.)

cause 80 percent lived with their children (Table 4-9). In the comparison countries, fewer of the aged lived with their children, but more in separate households saw their children frequently, so that about two-thirds of the total saw their children daily or almost daily. Less than 10 percent of the aged in both Japan and the comparison countries saw their children less than once a month. The big difference between Japan and the comparison countries, which increases the frequency of contact with children among the older Japanese, is the much greater proportion living with their children.

With such frequent contact, we might expect that few of the aged often feel lonely, despite widespread speculation to the contrary. In fact, less than 10 percent of the aged in all four countries say they often feel lonely and this proportion is only 4 percent in Japan (Table 4-10). Eighty-six percent of the older Japanese are rarely or never lonely. This too is probably related to the high proportion living with their children.

Also, almost all the older Japanese aged (96 percent)

Table 4-9. Most aged see their children at least every month (percentage distribution)

Time Frequency	Japan	U. S.	Britain	Denmark
Every day or every other day	85	63	69	62
Every week	4	18	17	22
Every month	5	7	8	10
Less than every month	6	10	6	6
Total	100	100	100	100

Source: Japan—estimated from number of contacts with relatives, National Life Center, 1972; other countries estimated from last time child seen, Shanas and associates, 1968. ("Every Day" includes those who live in joint households with a child.)

Table 4-10. Few aged often feel lonely (percentage distribution)

Feeling	Japan	U. S.	Britain	Denmark
Often lonely	4	9	7	4
Sometimes	10	21	21	13
Rarely or never	86	70	72	83
Total	100	100	100	100

Source: Japan—estimated from responses of those living alone on assumption that most living with children are rarely lonely, National Life Center, 1972; other countries—Shanas and associates, 1968.

said there is someone to care for them during illness or other emergency (Office of the Prime Minister, 1973), although this proportion drops to 78 percent among persons in Tokyo not living with a child (Tokyo Metropolitan Government, 1971). In the majority of cases, it is a child, grandchild, or daughter-in-law who would care for them, but other relatives, neighbors, or a maid are named by a total of 10 percent.

INSTITUTIONS

Another striking difference between Japan and the comparison nations is how few of the aged are living in institutions. While some countries have over 8 percent of their aged in long-term institutions, Japan has only 1 percent (Table 4-11).

The important question is whether this is the result of low demand for institutionalization of the aged or because of a shortage of facilities? In other words, do the Japanese believe that only one percent of the aged need institutionalization or do they want to quadruple the proportion in institutions? Opinion is divided on this issue. My impression is that most social workers and gerontologists in

Japan believe there is a terrible shortage of institutions and want to increase them drastically to levels comparable to most other industrialized countries (although probably not to the level in Finland with its rate of over 8 percent). They point to the long waiting lists for beds in most present institutions and to the fact that most nursing homes are not even accepting any more new applicants. On the other side, most government officials apparently believe that a moderate increase would be sufficient, given other more pressing needs. The present government five-year plan hopes to double the number of beds by 1976, but because the number of aged is increasing so rapidly, this would not raise the percent of the aged in institutions to even 2 percent. Government officials tend to favor paying a subsidy to households with bedfast aged, increasing the number of home helpers, and other policies to reduce the demand for institutionalization.

The evidence from surveys is also conflicting. Two surveys found that 3 percent of those over 65 said they wanted to get into an institution for the aged "now" (Ministry of Health and Welfare, 1970 and 1972b), but the most recent

Table 4-11. Japan has less institutionalized aged than other countries (percentage distribution of aged 65 and over)

	In Instituions
Finland	8.6
Norway	5.4
Denmark	5.3
Sweden	4.8
Britain	4.5
United States	3.7
Japan	1.0

Source: *Welfare Journal,* 1971.

survey found only 1 percent want to enter immediately (Office of the Prime Minister, 1973).

It seems likely that for the foreseeable future the strong tradition of keeping aged parents in joint households, even when they become bedfast, will continue to keep the proportion of Japanese aged in institutions at levels far below those of other industrialized countries. Another piece of evidence to support this view is the fact that Japan is rapidly increasing the number of home helpers for the aged even though she already has about five times as many as the United States relative to her population (Ministry of Health and Welfare, 1970).

This low rate of institutionalization is relevant to current efforts in the United States to prevent institutionalization of the aged and to reduce the numbers of aged already in institutions (Palmore, 1972b).

SUMMARY

The aged in Japan are more integrated into their families than the aged in the comparison industrialized countries. More than three-fourths actually live with their children, and this is true of all age groups and most areas. Whereas about half the single aged in the comparison countries live by themselves, in Japan there are very few single aged living by themselves. This is primarily due to preference rather than the housing shortage, financial necessity, or demographic differences. The aged perform many valued functions in the household. Living with children also seems to contribute to greater life satisfaction. Even among those who live in separate households, the majority live within 30 minutes travel of their nearest child and about half see their children at least every week. Fewer of the aged in Japan say they are often lonely than in the comparison countries, and this proportion will probably not increase much in the foreseeable future. Similarly, while there has been a small decline in the proportions living with their children, the data suggest that the vast majority will continue to live with their children.

Thus, the theory that industrialization causes a marked decline in the integration of the aged seems to have little relevance to the integration of older Japanese with their families. On the contrary, the theory that cultural traditions have important effects independent of economic factors is here demonstrated. The Japanese tradition of filial responsibility and respect for the aged seems to be the main force maintaining integration of the aged in their families despite the counterforces of industrialization.

5
Work and Retirement

Will these gnarled hands
keep pushing, pulling, pounding,
or fold and retire?

INDUSTRIALIZATION AND EMPLOYMENT

Perhaps the major decision faced by most aged in industrialized countries is whether to work or not to work. The results of this decision not only affect their income, but may affect their entire life-style and perhaps their health and longevity as well (Palmore, 1972a).

Again, Japan is fundamentally different from the comparison industrialized countries. Well over half the aged men in Japan continue to work, compared to less than a third in the United States and Britain (Table 5-1). Despite Japan's high degree of industrialization (see p. 13), her labor force participation rate for men over 65 is about half again as high as the average for all industrialized countries. Also the rate of employment among older Japanese is relatively high in all parts of the country, even though the proportion employed is about 5 percent higher in rural than in urban areas (Office of the Prime Minister, 1973). The rate of employment may have declined some recently, as a result of the energy crisis, but it probably remains much higher than in other industrialized countries.

This is another major piece of evidence that the integration of the aged can remain high despite industrialization; the facts are clear that the integration of the aged in the work force has remained high in Japan relative to that of other industrialized countries. This seems to have resulted from two complementary traditions. One tradition is the feeling in Japan, especially among the aged, that every able person should work as much and as long as possible. Those who continue to work are generally more respected than those who do not. This feeling is reflected in the present low level of social security benefits for the retired (see Chapter 4).

This tradition may appear to be contradicted by the fact that the customary "retirement age" in most businesses is about age 55. But, in Japan, "retirement" at age 55 usually means simply switching to another company, to another job in the same company, or to self-employment (see p. 57-59). Ninety-six per cent of men aged 55-59 continue

Table 5-1. More of the aged in Japan are in the labor force (percentage distribution)

| | Over Age 65 in the Labor Force | |
Country	Men	Women
Japan	55	18
United States	32	13
Britain	28	8
Denmark	38	8
Average for countries that are:		
Industrialized	38	—
Semi-industrialized	61	—
Agricultural	70	—

Source: Japan—Census Bureau, 1965; U. S., Britain, and Denmark—Shanas and associates, 1968; averages by industrialization—United Nations, 1962 (data for 1950's).

to work and 78 percent of those 60-69 also continue to work (Office of the Prime Minister, 1973).

The other tradition is that of seniority and respect for the aged which appears to prevent discrimination against the aged in employment, such as is found in other industrialized countries (Palmore, 1972a). The aged in Japan appear to have more opportunities for employment. Less than 10 percent of employers surveyed said they were "dissatisfied" with the speed, skill, diligence, efficiency, or human relations of older workers (National Life Center, 1972).

THE EMPLOYED

Who are the employed aged? What do they do? How much do they work? Why do they work? These are all questions relevant to the status and integration of the aged into the work force. We will discuss primarily working men, because in Japan, as elsewhere, there are relatively few employed aged women (Table 5-1).

To begin with age, in both age groups 65-69 and 70 plus, more Japanese men work than do American men (Table 5-2). Yet the majority of the employed older men in Japan are still under 70 (Table 5-3). This is in contrast to the

Table 5-2. More older Japanese men are in the labor force than older American men, both over and under 70 (percentage distribution of men in labor force)

Age	Japan	U. S.
65-69	77	44
70+	40	22

Source: Japan, Office of the Prime Minister, 1973; United States, 1960 Census.

Table 5-3. Aged workers in Japan tend to be younger than in other countries (percentage distribution of employed men by age)

Age	Japan	U. S.	Britain	Denmark
65-69	60	37	41	38
70-74	27	32	30	28
75-79	10	17	15	19
80+	3	14	14	15
Total	100	100	100	100

Japan source: 1965 Census.

comparison countries where a minority of the employed older men are under 70.

As for what they do, over two-thirds are self-employed or work in the family business (Table 5-4). This is in contrast to the United States where only a third are self-employed or unpaid family workers (Epstein and Murray, 1967, Table 7-9). As for occupation, over half are farmers, lumbermen, or fishermen (Table 5-5), in contrast to the United States where only 20 percent of the men and 6 per-

Table 5-4. The majority of older workers in Japan are self-employed or help in family business (1968) (percentage distribution)

Aged	Self-employed	Work in Family Business	Regular Employees	Part-time Employees	Other
Men:					
65-69	54	11	26	6	3
70-74	51	17	23	6	3
75+	51	25	14	7	2
Women:					
65-69	27	52	7	7	8
70-74	19	59	5	5	13
75+	39	44	4	6	7

Source: National Life Center, 1972.

Table 5-5. The majority of the older Japanese workers are farmers (percentage distribution)

Occupation	Workers 15-64	Workers 65+
Professional and technical	6	4
Managers and officials	3	5
Clerical	13	3
Sales	12	14
Farmers, lumbermen, fishermen	23	55
Transportation	5	—
Craftsmen, operatives, and laborers	31	14
Service workers	7	4
Total	100	100

Source: 1965 Japan Census.

cent of the women are in agriculture (Epstein and Murray, 1967, Table 7.9). Also twice as many of the older Japanese as of the older Americans work in sales occupations. Thus, in Japan there are many more opportunities for older persons to remain or become self-employed farmers or shopkeepers than in the United States. In rural Japan these older farmers are much in evidence toiling in their rice paddies or vegetable gardens with straw "coolie" hats to protect them from the weather. The older shopkeeper tending his or her little specialty shop is also a common sight. There are also many traditional occupations in which older persons are often at the peak of their career.

Painters, writers, actors, and certain highly skilled artisans often do not achieve full competence until their middle or late fifties 'and many pursue active professional lives far into the seventies and even eighties. Great respect is accorded these people, even by the very young in the same profession (Smith, 1961).

These opportunities for older workers are another reason for the greater integration of the older Japanese in the labor force.

As for how much they work, some retire to part-time jobs and some increase their hours of work to make up for reduced earnings, but the overall average number of hours worked is about the same for wage and salary workers over age 60 as for other workers: about 48 hours per week (Table 5-6). It is probable that many self-employed workers also work long hours, especially on farms and in family shops. Japanese older workers appear to put in more hours than older workers in other industrialized countries. In the United States, Great Britain, and Denmark, the average number of hours for blue-collar workers over age 65 is less than 40 hours per week (Shanas and associates, 1968, p. 304). Thus, not only do more of the older Japanese continue to work, but they work longer hours as well.

Why do the older Japanese continue to work so much? How many continue to work because of financial necessity and how many work for other reasons? It is difficult to get valid and reliable data on this question because many people work for a mixture of motivations, and the stated reasons are often influenced by rationalization and the social acceptability of various answers. Nevertheless, the findings of several surveys agree that less than half of all older workers continue to work primarily because of financial necessity. For example, one recent survey of all

Table 5-6. Older Japanese workers work as many hours but earn less income than younger workers

	Average Hours Worked Per Month	Average Total Annual Earnings (Yen)
All wage and salary workers	206	639,000
Wage and salary workers over age 60	207	579,000

Source: Ministry of Health and Welfare, 1970.

workers over 60 found that the most frequent reason given for working was "duty," while financial necessity was given by a little over one-third (Table 5-7). Even fewer of the workers in the primary industries gave financial necessity as the primary reason. Another survey which allowed multiple answers found similar percentages giving financial necessity, but many more who said they wanted to continue working because it was enjoyable (28 percent) or because it was healthy (44 percent) (Office of the Prime Minister, 1973). Here again is the problem of bias toward socially desirable answers. Perhaps a more objective way to get at this is to ask whether the earnings are used for primary support or for secondary support, luxuries, and such extras. The answers to this question indicate that less than half work to provide primary support while the majority provide secondary support, luxuries, or other things (Table 5-8). A survey in which workers of all ages were asked what was their attitude toward work after retirement found about half who said that work after retirement is "normal" and only 7 percent who said they would work only if it was financially necessary (National Life Center, 1972). A survey of men over 50 found that

Table 5-7. Reasons for working among all Japanese workers over 60 (percentage distribution)

Reasons	Total	Primary Industries	Secondary Industries	Other Regular Workers	Day Laborers
Duty	41	47	31	36	38
Financial necessity	36	29	50	51	51
Enjoyable or healthy	17	20	17	8	5
Other	5	4	2	4	—
Total	100	100	100	100	100

Source: Ministry of Health and Welfare, 1970.

Table 5-8. Use of earnings among older Japanese workers (percentages distribution)

Use	Total 60 +	Men	Women
Primary support	43	54	23
Secondary support	33	27	45
Luxuries	8	6	10
Pocket money	6	5	9
Other	10	8	14
Total	100	100	100

Source: Ministry of Health and Welfare, 1972.

83 percent said that it is better to work as long as possible rather than retire from work, and there was little variation in this percent by age, area, or education (Office of the Prime Minister, 1973).

I know of no comparable data in Western countries, but I expect that many more, perhaps most, American workers over 65 would say they work because of financial necessity. There would be few older Americans who would say they work because of duty, because it is healthy, or because it is "normal" to work after retirement. The fact that few Americans do work after retirement shows that most consider it "normal" to *stop* work at retirement. One piece

Table 5-9. More of the Japanese workers want to continue working (percentage distribution)

Attitudes Toward Work	Japanese Over 65	U. S. Over 65
Want to continue work	91	70
Want to stop work	4	19
Undecided	5	11
Total	100	100

Source: Japan—*Welfare Journal,* 1971; U. S.—Epstein and Murray, 1967.

of comparable evidence is that most of the older Japanese workers want to continue working, while 30 percent of older American workers plan to stop working next year or are undecided (Table 5-9). In summary, the "work ethic" appears to be stronger among older Japanese than among the aged in other industrialized countries, and the majority of the aged in Japan continue to work for reasons other than financial necessity.

SOME ILLUSTRATIONS

There are many Japanese stories which illustrate the expectations that older persons should continue to work as long as possible. One of the most famous classic stories is that of an old couple in the "Slittongue Sparrow." The old man is rewarded for befriending a lost sparrow and for his lack of greed; the old woman is punished for cutting the tongue of the sparrow and for her greed. But the point for present purposes is that, although both were quite old, the man continued working as a wood-cutter and the woman continued to do all the housework, as is normal for most older Japanese.

A more recent story is that of "Old Gen" whose attempt to adopt a son ends tragically, but who continues to earn his living rowing passengers to and from his island up until the day of his death (Keene, 1956).

A modern story is about Miike Shuntaro, a 78-year-old research scientist in anatomy, who considers suicide but concludes, "Man was meant to work furiously to the end. Why else was he created? Not to bask in the sun, surely. Not just to be happy" (Inoue, 1960, p. 138). And so he returns from viewing "The Azaleas of Hira" to finish his several volumes on the "Arterial System of the Japanese."

Another modern story involves a grandmother, Osumi, who sometimes wishes that her widowed daughter-in-law, Otami, would remarry so that Otami could stay home and help with the housework. Otami wants to remain a widow in order to save their land for her son. During a heated argument, Otami says to Osumi, "If you don't want to work, you have no choice but to die" (Akutagawa, 1961, p. 93).

There are a few stories about retired Japanese (see Chapter 7), but these are all about very senile and incapacitated elders. These are the "exceptions which prove the rule" that older Japanese are usually expected to continue doing at least some work as long as they are able.

RETIREMENT

"Retirement" can mean several rather different things. It can mean that the older person has stopped all gainful employment, or it can mean that the older worker has retired from regular employment and now works part-time or occasionally, or it can mean that the older worker has retired from his usual job but is still working as much or more than he ever did (Palmore, 1971). In the United States, the great majority of retired men fit the first meaning. Earlier we showed that in Japan most men continue to work at least until age 70 despite "retirement" at age 55. About half the "retired" men continue to do the same type job, either in a different company or on a somewhat reduced basis in the same company; about a quarter shift to a somewhat different kind of job; and the other quarter move to an entirely different type job (National Life Center, 1972). We will use retirement in the more general sense of change from usual or regular job regardless of whether the person continues to work or not. When we want to refer specifically to those no longer working we will use the term "not employed."

The most frequent retirement age among wage and salary workers is age 55, although about a quarter of surveyed firms have compulsory ages over 60 (National Life Center, 1972). About three-fourths of all industries (and nearly all large firms) have a compulsory retirement system. However, 82 percent of the companies with a compulsory retirement age also have various exceptions and ways of getting around the "compulsory" retirement, such as provisions for creating a new job not subject to compulsory retirement, extending the old job temporarily, or offering a job with reduced pay and changed conditions of employment. The pattern of "permanent employment" in most Japanese firms motivates them to provide some kind of employment for their older workers even after "compulsory retirement" (Cole, 1973; Abegglen, 1958).

Workers who "retire" to another job have a drop in earnings of about one-fourth on the average. If they stay in the same company, it drops less (17 percent) and if they move to another company it drops more (33%) (National Life Center, 1972). There is considerable talk and some action toward moving the usual retirement age up to 60 or beyond. A survey of workers found that two-thirds said age 55 was too young to retire; over half favored retirement at age 60 or beyond (National Life Center, 1972). The two most frequent arguments for raising the usual retirement age are that the nation needs to utilize more fully the skills and potential productivity of older persons, and that because of current low levels of retirement benefits many older persons need continued employment for a decent standard of living.

Professor Peter Drucker, on the other hand, believes that the Japanese system of retirement at age 55 make labor costs more flexible and is one factor in "Japan's economic miracle." He argues that since most retired workers become "temporary" workers at reduced pay who may be laid off if there is not enough work, these workers reduce labor costs and make them more flexible. He also says that, because most firms have programs of continuous training and retraining, worker productivity rises with age so that older workers are more productive than younger workers. He says Japanese studies show that output per man-hour is almost always considerably higher in plants with an older employee population (Drucker, 1971).

Reasons for not working are just as difficult to assess as the reasons for continued employment discussed earlier. Nevertheless, the available data indicate that in Japan there are less older men who want to work but are unable to get jobs than in the comparison industrialized countries (Table 5-10). Conversely, in Japan more of the older un-

Table 5-10. Reasons for not working in Japan, United States, Great Britain, and Denmark (percentage distribution of retired men)

Reasons	Japan	U. S.	Britain	Denmark
Bad health; felt too old	42	50	44	61
Forced to retire; want work	6	29	32	17
Voluntary reasons	52	21	23	23
Total	100	100	100	100

Source: Japan—not-employed men over 60, Ministry of Health and Welfare, 1970; other countries—not employed men over 65, Shanas and associates, 1968. (Results from these two sources are not exactly comparable because somewhat different questions and response categories were used, but they are similar enough for present purposes of rough comparison.)

employed men are no longer working because of various voluntary reasons. This difference in reasons for not working is probably another reflection of the greater job opportunities for older men in Japan. To put it another way, greater job opportunities tend to decrease involuntary retirement and increase the proportion voluntarily retired.

TRENDS

But what of the future? Is the present high level of integration of older Japanese in the work force a temporary phenomenon which will rapidly decline in the near future? Forecasting the future is a hazardous undertaking in any field, but based on recent trends it seems probable that there will continue to be only small declines in the employment of the aged. On the other hand, better pensions may cause a greater decline than in the past.

Compared to the United States, the aged in Japan have experienced relatively little decline in labor force participation since 1930 (Table 5-11). While the labor force partici-

Table 5-11. Labor force participation rates of older Japanese has declined relatively little since 1930 (percentage distribution in labor force)

Age	1930		1965	
	Japan	U. S.	Japan	U. S.
Total 65+	38	30	34	17
Men	63	54	55	27
Women	19	7	18	9
Total 15-64	72	55	69	67
Men	88	85	86	89
Women	52	24	53	44

Source: 1930 and 1965, Japan Census; 1930 U. S. Census and 1965 Current Population Survey.

pation of older Americans was cut in half, that of older Japanese declined only four percentage points, which is about the same decline experienced by the nonaged in Japan. It is true that the older Japanese men experienced somewhat more decline (8 percentage points), but this is much less than the precipitous drop experienced by older American men (27 percentage points). This contrast becomes even more impressive when it is noted that the labor force participation of the nonaged Americans had a marked *increase* during this period (12 percentage points).

A more systematic way of looking at trends in the employment status of the aged is the use the Equality Index (EI) to compare the relative similarity of the aged to the nonaged in terms of labor force participation, occupational and industrial distribution. As explained in the Methods section (Chapter 1), the EI is a comprehensive measure of the similarity between any two groups that can be used with any type of data. In the present analysis the two groups are the aged (age 65 and over) and the nonaged adults (ages 15-64). For the labor force EI we use the percentage of each group in the labor force; for the occupation EI we use the percentage distributions of employed persons in the eight standard Japanese Census occupations (see Table 5-5); and for the industry EI we use the percentage distributions of employed persons in primary, secondary, and tertiary industries. The EI for the United States were computed in a similar way, except that the occupation EI is based on the eleven categories of the U. S. Census and the industry EI is based on the eight categories in the U. S. Census. Table 5-12 shows the results of this analysis.

As might be expected from the relatively small decline in labor force participation among older Japanese, the

Table 5-12. Trends in Equality Indexes for Japan and United States in labor force, occupation, and industry (age 65 and compared to ages 15-65)

Category	Past	Present	Annual Change
Japan:			
Labor Force	66(1930)	65(1965)	−.03
Occupation	69(1950)	63(1965)	−.40
Industry	65(1960)	70(1970)	+.50
United States:			
Labor Force	75(1930)	50(1965)	−.71
Occupation	79(1950)	76(1965)	−.20
Industry	87(1940)	79(1970)	−.27

Source: Japan Census for 1930, 1950, 1960, 1965 and 1970; United States Census for 1930, 1940, 1950, 1965 and 1970.

labor force EI for Japan shows almost no decline since 1930. In contrast, the labor force EI in the United States has declined by 25 points. Projected into the future, this would mean that the labor force participation of older Japanese would not fall much more below that of other Japanese, while that of older Americans would begin to approach zero by the end of the century.

The occupation EI in Japan and the United States show similar moderate declines (an annual decline of 0.4 in Japan and 0.2 in the United States). Projected into the future this would mean that in both Japan and the United States the older workers will continue to be left behind in the older occupations such as farming and small shopkeepers while the nonaged move more into the newer occupations such as service workers. Since the older occupations tend to be lower in socio-economic status, this would mean a general decline in relative socio-economic status for the aged still employed. However, it should be noted that this trend is based on only a 15-year interval (occupation in Japan by age was unavailable prior to 1950), which may reflect only a short-term fluctuation rather than a long-term trend. For example, the occupation EI in the United States actually increased between 1940 and 1965 (Palmore and Whittington, 1971).

The industry EI for Japan is based on an even shorter interval (1960-1970), and may also reflect only a short-term fluctuation, but is is of interest because it is the only EI which shows an increase. The industry EI in the United States shows the expected long-term decline of eight points since 1940.

In summary, this analysis indicates that the relative situation of older Japanese is not declining in terms of labor force participation nor in type of industry, but is declining moderately in terms of occupation; while the situation of the older Americans is declining in all three areas and this decline is especially steep in labor force participation.

INTERNATIONAL CORRELATIONS[1]

Another way to estimate future trends in the employment of older Japanese is to look at other countries to see if there is general association between industrialization and status of the aged in terms of employment and occupation. If there is a strong linear correlation, this would be a basis for predicting a decline in the relative employment and occupation status of older Japanese in so far as Japan continues to become more industrialized. If there is a strong curvilineal association, this would be a basis for different predictions, depending on Japan's present position on the curve.

[1]Most of the material in this section comes from an analysis published in Palmore and Manton, 1974.

In exploring the relationship between modernization and economic status of the aged we used several indicators of modernization. The gross national product per capita was used to measure the increased productivity that results from industrialization. The present degree of industrialization is most directly measured by the percent of the labor force engaged in agriculture. The *rate* of industrialization was measured by the percent annual change in the proportion of the labor force engaged in agriculture. Since increased education is associated with modernization and indirectly with industrialization we analyzed three indicators of education: percent of adults who are literate, percent of people aged 5–19 who are in school, and percent of the population who are in higher education. Data for these statistics came from Russett, 1964, and refer to the period around 1960.

To measure the relative employment status of the aged we used the categories of "economically active" and "not economically active" to compute the EI of persons 65 and over, compared to those of age 25 through 64. The occupation EI was computed using the ten major categories given in the UN Demographic Yearbook (1964 and 1965). We were able to find sufficient data to compute the EI in 24 countries or territories (Table 5-13). We excluded a few very small countries or territories from this analysis both because of the small number of aged and because they may be untypical of most other countries.

The EI's on employment and occupation range from high scores in the eighties (and one of 92) for such non-industrialized countries such as El Salvador, the Phillipines, Iraq, and Iran to low scores in the fifties for such industrialized countries as Canada and the United States (Table 5-13). This shows that there is a general negative association between industrialization and economic status of the aged relative to the nonaged: the more industrialized countries have less employment for the aged, and the employed aged tend to be concentrated in the older occupations.

In order to examine more precisely what indicators of modernization were most closely associated with economic status of the aged, we first did simple zero-order correlations of each of the six modernization indicators

Table 5-13. Employment and occupation equality indexes of aged and non-aged in 24 countries

Country	Employment EI	Occupation EI
Canada	53	77
Chile	73	77
Costa Rica	74	81
El Salvador	84	92
Ghana	80	82
Greece	61	72
Honduras	79	89
Hungary	67	54
Iraq	88	78
Iran	86	89
Ireland	73	68
Japan	65	70
Korea	64	80
Malaysia	71	86
Netherlands	60	74
New Zealand	53	84
Norway	63	78
Panama	71	78
Philippines	84	84
Portugal	77	74
Puerto Rico	62	75
Sweden	51	77
Taiwan	54	78
United States	54	79

Source: United Nations, 1964 and 1965.

with each of the two economic status EI's.[1] Table 5-14 shows that gross national product has a strong negative correlation with the employment EI (-0.79), but little correlation with the occupation EI. This suggests that increased productivity tends to decrease employment of the aged (or possibly vice versa), but has little effect on the occupation status of the aged. As for the shift from agriculture, the percentage of the labor force in agriculture is very strongly correlated with the employment EI (0.91) and moderately correlated with occupation EI. This indicates that in most countries the relative employment status of the aged can be mostly explained by the percentage in agriculture: the less in agriculture, the more retirement and unemployment among the aged. On the other hand, the annual percentage change in proportion of the labor force

Table 5-14. Countries of modernization indicators and equality indexes (N=No. of Countries)

Modernization Indicator	Employment EI	(N)	Occupation EI	(N)
GNP/per capita	−.79	(22)	−.16	(23)
% in agriculture	.91	(22)	.45	(23)
% change in agriculture	.12	(17)	.29	(16)
% adults literate	−.80	(22)	−.57	(23)
% age 5-19 in school	−.85	(22)	−.58	(23)
% in higher education	−.55	(22)	−.23	(23)

Source: Modernization Indication from Russett, 1964.

[1]Hungary was omitted from the Occupation EI correlations because it was found to lie more than 4 standard deviations away from its predicted position, apparently because of massive changes in occupations among younger adults since it became a communist nation. Also, Taiwan and South Korea were omitted from the Employment EI correlations because they lay more than 4 standard deviations away from their predicted positions, presumably because of the recent civil wars. Exclusion of these countries did not affect the overall pattern, but did increase the correlations substantially.

in agriculture has only weak correlations with the two EI's. We suspect that this is because of a time-lag problem: the current EI are probably affected more by the rate of change in agriculture a generation or two ago, rather than by current rates of change. Of the three measures of education, the percentage of youths who are in school is more strongly related to both EI's than are the other two measures.

However, when we plotted these indicators of modernization against the EI, we noted that many of the relationships seemed to be "J" shaped: in the underdeveloped countries the EI decline with early modernization, but then the EI seem to level off and begin to rise up in the most modernized countries. Therefore, we tried fitting a quadratic curve to the relationships: that is, we used the quadratic equation of $Y = a + bX + cX_2$; where Y is the EI, a is a constant, b is the linear coefficient, c is coefficient of the squared term, and X is the indicator of modernization. The predicted curve from such a quadratic equation is "J" shaped and did substantially improve the variance explained over that of the simple correlation for several of the relationships.

Specifically, we tested to see if the variance explained by the best linear correlation of each EI could be significantly improved by using a quadratic equation. The simple linear correlation of percentage in agriculture with the employment EI was so high that the quadratic equation did not significantly improve the variance explained (Figure 5-1). However, the quadratic equation for percentage of youths in school against the occupation EI did improve the variance explained (r^2) from 0.34 to 0.40 (Figure 5-2). This improvement was statistically significant at the 0.10 level. An even clearer example of a "J" shaped relationship is that between gross national product

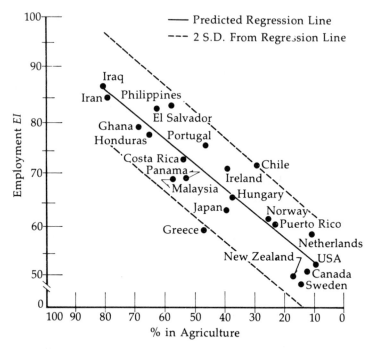

Figure 5-1. *Percentage in agriculture and employment EI* ($r^2 = 0.83$)

and employment EI (Figure 5-3). In this case the variance explained was increased from 0.62 to 0.79 by use of the quadratic equation, and the increase was statistically significant at 0.001 level.

It should be noted that all the countries in all three figures are within or near two standard deviations (dotted lines) from the predicted regression line (solid line). This indicates that, except for the three countries noted in the previous footnote (Hungary, Taiwan, South Korea), there are no countries which deviate much from the general pattern of strong relationships between modernization and status of the aged.

We believe the most interesting aspect of this analysis

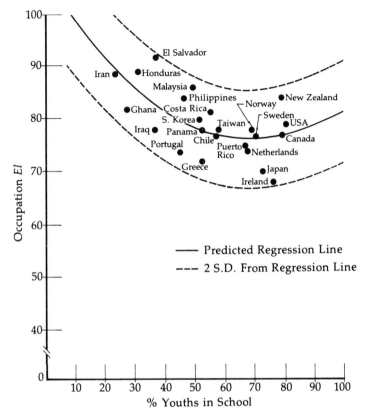

Figure 5-2. *Percentage of youths in school and occupation EI (r² = 0.40)*

is the discovery of the "J" shaped relationships presented in Figures 5-2 and 5-3. These relationships imply that the relative economic status of the aged decreases in the early stages of modernization; but that, after a country has gone through a rapid period of modernization, these aspects of status stabilize and may begin to rise. The most obvious explanation for this reversal is that, during the early stages of modernization, the greatest changes which produce the greatest discrepancies between the aged and nonaged

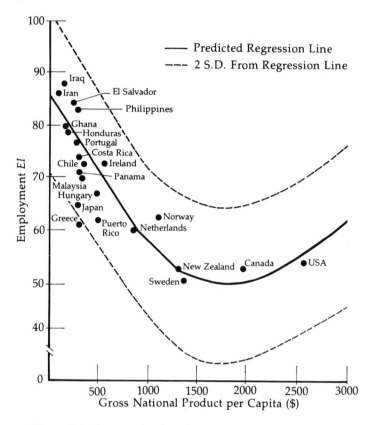

Figure 5-3. *Gross national product per capita and employment EI ($r^2 = 0.79$)*

occur, but that when societies "mature" the rates of change (in agriculture and education) level off and the discrepancies between aged and nonaged decrease. There may be other factors such as the growth of new institutions to replace the farm and family in maintaining the status of the aged such as retirement benefits, more adult education and job retraining, policies against age discrimination in employment, etc.

Specifically, Japan's position on these J-shaped curves suggests that her occupation EI may begin to rise with further increases in education (see Figure 5-2) and that her employment EI may decline somewhat with increase gross national product, but then level off and begin to increase (Figure 5-3).

SUMMARY

Japan is fundamentally different from other industrialized countries in terms of integration of the aged in the work force. Almost twice as many of the aged men continue to work in Japan as in the comparison industrialized countries. This seems to have resulted from two traditions: duty to work and respect for the aged which reduces discrimination in the employment of the aged. Compared to these other industrialized countries, more of the older Japanese workers are self-employed or work in the family business, more are farmers or in sales occupations (primarily small shopkeepers), and they continue to work longer hours. The majority appear to work for reasons such as a sense of duty, enjoyment, or health rather than because of financial necessity. In Japan usually "retirement" simply means reduced pay, loss of seniority, different job, or less hours at the same job rather than complete cessation of work.

Most of the older Japanese who are no longer working have stopped for voluntary and health reasons, rather than because of compulsory retirement and other discriminations against the aged. Based on past trends and analysis of Equality Indexes, it seems probable that there will continue to be only small declines in labor force participation and other indicators of the relative economic status of the aged. There is even the possibility, suggested by international correlations showing curvilinear relationships between modernization and economic status, that the status of older Japanese may level off and begin to increase in the future. Thus, in the area of employment, Japan again demonstrates that the status and integration of the aged can remain relatively high despite industrialization.

6
Income
and Support

The "Golden Years" may
seem to glow, glitter, and shine;
yet have little gold.

The financial situation of older Japanese is probably the
weakest part of their.current status. Few have adequate
pensions, social security benefits, or other independent
sources of income. Yet a cross-cultural evaluation of their
financial situation is difficult for several reasons. First, few
current nation-wide data exist on income of the older Japanese. There are data on income of households headed by
older Japanese, but these include the income of younger
persons in the household and do not represent the majority
of older Japanese living in households headed by their
children. Furthermore, since about three-fourths of older
Japanese live with their children, it is difficult to tell the extent to which they are dependent on their children for food
and shelter or to which they "pay their own way" through
household functions such as child care and housekeeping.
Finally, the way of life and standard of living in Japan are
so different from that of the comparison industrialized
countries that comparing dollar values of cash income becomes a poor indicator of the actual adequacy of resources.

INHERITANCE AND SUPPORT FROM CHILDREN

Before World War II, legal requirements and social norms prescribing the duty of the eldest son to support his parents and his corresponding right to inherit all of his parents' property combined to assure a minimal support for most older Japanese. Although there were some exceptions to this pattern, the system provided a form of "social security" for older Japanese. When there was not a son in the family, a *mukoyoshi* (adopted husband) was usually adopted into the family to fulfil the functions of the oldest son.

After World War II, this system was modified so that there is now usually more division of the inheritance among all the children. The present standard regulation is that, if there is no will specifying otherwise, one-third of the father's estate goes to the wife and the other two-thirds is divided equally among the children. When the mother dies, her estate is also divided equally among the children. However, a will can be drawn bequeathing up to half of the father's estate any way the father desires, but the other half must be divided according to the above formula. Therefore, if a father wishes to favor his oldest son, he can bequeath up to half his estate to the oldest son plus the required portion of the other half. The mother can do the same thing, so that the oldest son still can inherit the bulk of the estate if he has only one or two siblings. In fact, the oldest son still is most likely to be the main child caring for his parents and, because of this, is most likely to inherit more of the parents' estate than the other children. Thus, the traditional system has not been abolished but only modified.

Along with this shift in inheritance patterns, there appears to be a shift toward more Japanese believing that pensions or social security, rather than children, should become the primary support for the aged. Half the older Japanese still say that the family should be responsible for support of the aged, but less than a third of younger Japanese agree with this (Table 6-1). Also, there has been a marked shift between 1966 and 1971 away from the belief that the "aged themselves" should be responsible for their support and toward the belief that the "nation" (through pensions and social security) should be responsible (Table 6-1). This reflects the growing strength of the pension and social security system of retirement benefits (see pp. 83-89).

When we compare present Japanese beliefs about support of the aged with those of Americans (Table 6-2) there appears to be little difference remaining, although there are a few more Americans than Japanese favoring support by the nation and a few less Americans saying the aged themselves should be responsible. Also, there is little difference between older and younger Americans, except that somewhat more of the older Americans say the aged them-

Table 6-1. Attitudes of Japanese toward who should be responsible for support of aged are shifting from self and family to nation (percentage distribution)

Age	Year	Aged Themselves	Family	Nation	Don't Know
60+	1970	23	50	17	11
20+	1971	21	32	42	6
20+	1966	40	27	25	8

Source: Ministry of Health and Welfare, 1970; National Life Center, 1972. ("Nation" includes employer pensions and government social security and welfare.)

Table 6-2. Attitudes of older and younger Americans show similar shift toward responsibility for support of the aged (1957 percentage distribution)

Age	Aged Themselves	Family	Nation	Other; No Answer
65+	24	26	45	5
21+	17	33	48	2

Source: Shanas, 1962 (adapted). ("Nation" includes employer pensions and government social security and welfare.)

selves should be responsible. This may indicate a continuing shift in America (as in Japan) away from the idea that the aged should be self-sufficient.

However, when adult younger Japanese with living parents are asked who would *actually* provide support if their parents needed it, most say that they themselves or their siblings would provide the support for their parents (Table 6-3). This is a more accurate reflection of actual support patterns than are the beliefs about who *should* (ideally) support older people, which were discussed in the above paragraphs. Adult, non-aged Japanese saying they would support their parents constitute a similar percentage in rural areas and in all cities—except Tokyo where more

Table 6-3. Most Japanese aged would be supported by their children if they needed support (percentage distribution)

Area	Children	Institution	Other
Tokyo	78	13	9
6 other large cities	86	2	12
Other cities of 100,000+	92	2	6
Cities of less than 100,000	90	3	7
Rural	87	3	10
Average for all Japan	89	4	7

Source: National Life Center, 1972.

say that an institution would support their parents. The latter may reflect a greater availability of institutions for the aged in Tokyo than in other areas.

Yet, the actual support patterns show that the aged are shifting away from being dependent on their families for support and are becoming more self-sufficient by employment, pensions, and assets (Table 6-4). In 1968, the self-sufficient aged were still in the minority (38 percent), but the trend indicates that they soon will be in the majority.

Table 6-4. Older Japanese are becoming less dependent on family support and more self-sufficient (percentage distribution of 65+)

	1957	1968
Self-sufficient by employment	18	25
Self-sufficient by pensions	2	9
Self-sufficient by assets and other	1	3
Total self-sufficient	21	38
Dependent on family	77	57
Dependent on public assistance	2	2
Dependent on other sources	—	3
Total dependent	79	62

Source: 1957 data, Ministry of Health and Welfare, 1970; 1968 data, National Life Center, 1972.

The continuing improvement in pensions and social security will probably be the main factors in this trend. This trend is also reflected in the fact that well over half the Japanese in their sixties were already self-sufficient in 1968, while relatively few over 70 were self-sufficient (Table 6-5).

Another way to look at self-sufficiency or dependency is to ask the older person whether he considers his income to be adequate or not. A recent survey found that four in

Table 6-5. Japanese in their 60's are more self-sufficient than those over 70 (percentage distribution in 1968)

	60-64	65-69	70-74	75-79	80+
Self-sufficient by employment	56	40	23	10	4
Self-sufficient by pensions	4	5	11	12	12
Self-sufficient by assets and other	4	5	3	3	2
Total self-sufficient	64	50	37	25	18
Dependent on family	32	45	58	69	77
Dependent on public assistance	1	2	3	2	1
Dependent on other sources	2	2	2	3	2
Total dependent	35	49	63	74	80
Unclear	1	1	1	1	2

Source: National Life Center, 1972.

Table 6-6. Few Japanese over 70 and few in rural areas have adequate incomes (1972) (percentage distribution)

	Adequate Incomes
Age:	
Total age 50+	38
Men 50-59	56
Men 60+	42
Men 70+	36
Women 50-59	40
Women 60+	20
Women 70+	15
Area:	
Tokyo	52
9 other large cities	38
Other cities 100,000+	43
Cities less than 100,000	38
Rural	29

Source: Office of the Prime Minister, 1973.

ten men over 60 and only two in ten women over 60 reported that they have adequate incomes. As expected, those over 70 and those in rural areas had even lower proportions reporting adequate incomes (Table 6-6).

Such surveys give us useful information about relative satisfaction with income, but little information about *actual* levels of income. Meager current national data on actual income of older Japanese exist, but a 1960 survey of Japanese over 65 (excluding the 24 percent who run their own business or are employed in their family business) found that most had annual incomes of less than $216 (Table 6-7). The average income for men was $217; for women it was only $73. In contrast, the median income of older American couples and single persons in 1967 was $1828 (Table 6-8). Although this latter figure in American economic terms is still in the poverty range, it is clearly more adequate than the average income of older Japanese.

Table 6-7. Most Japanese over 65 had less than $216 in 1960 (percentage distribution by annual income in dollars)

Annual Income ($)	Total 65 +	Men	Women
No Income	15	10	18
1-$71	53	42	59
72-215	21	25	18
216-359	4	7	2
360-719	4	8	1
720+	3	8	1
Amount unknown	1	1	1
Total	100	100	100
Mean income	$130	$217	$73

Source: Ministry of Health and Welfare, 1960. (Excluded are the 24% who run their own business or are employed in their family business because their net income is usually unknown. If their income were included, the average would be slightly higher.)

Table 6-8. Older Americans have more income than older Japanese (percentage distribution of U.S. aged units by income, 1967)

U.S. Aged Unit by Income	All Units	Couples	Non-married Men	Non-married Women
Less than $1000	21	3	20	36
$1000-$1999	33	17	41	42
$2000-$2999	17	23	22	12
$3000-$3999	10	19	7	4
$4000 or more	19	38	11	7
Median income	$1828	$3373	$1692	$1227

Source: Bixby, 1970. ("Aged units" are persons over 65 living alone or a couple with one or both over 65.)

Clearly, most older Japanese relied heavily on family support since they had such little income of their own.

PENSIONS

Perhaps the main reason for the low incomes of older Japanese is the inadequate pension system. It is true that all Japanese workers under age 60 are now covered by some kind of pension program. The Employee Pension Insurance (EPI) and other public employee plans cover about half the employed persons (22 million). The National Pension Insurance (NPI) covers most self-employed persons. The Non-contributory Old Age Pension covers all other persons who are over age 70 and have income of less than about $1500 per year. There are also many special employee pension plans and private pension schemes which supplement the basic compulsory programs.

The main problem currently in Japan is that only 7 percent of persons over age 65 in 1970 qualified for one of the contributory pension benefits (*Welfare Journal*, 1971). The

Non-contributory Old Age Pension pays only about $20.00 per month. This is only "pocket-money" and must be supplemented by public assistance unless there is some other means of support. The National Pension Insurance is also so new (1965) that few over 65 qualify for more than token amounts. Even the older and more adequate employee pension and public employee plans have wage replacement ratios that are much lower than comparable ones in the United States, Great Britain, or Denmark (Table 6-9).* As Japan's pension plans mature and more older Japanese qualify for beneifts based on a longer period of coverage, the adequacy of pensions will improve considerably. But this is no help for the present generation of older Japanese.

As a result of her presently low pension benefits, Japan spends much less per person over 65 on social security and welfare for the aged than other industrialized nations (Table 6-10). The country nearest to Japan in amount spent per person, France, spends two and a half times as much as Japan. The United States spends over five times as much per person as Japan. Even allowing for differences in stan-

Table 6-9. The wage replacement ratio of pensions is lowest in Japan

Wage Replacement Ratio	Japan	U. S.	Britain	Denmark
Current average EPI pension for couple as percent of average wage	19	29	29	40
Current average EPI pension for couple as percent of GNP per person in labor force	12	21	22	29

Source: Japan—Fisher, 1973 (data for 1970-71); other countries—Shanas and associates, 1968 (data for 1962).

*All benefits in Japan were at least doubled in September, 1973.

Table 6-10. The Japanese Government spends less on the aged than other industrialized nations (1964-67)

Country	Annual Amount Spent Per Person 65 + By Social Security and Welfare
West Germany	$978
United States	942
Sweden	795
Britain	486
Italy	447
France	432
Japan	174

Source: National Life Center, 1972.

dard of living, it is clear that Japan is far behind other industrialized nations in social security for the aged.

Another way of looking at Japan's effort to provide adequate incomes for her aged is to compare her social security expenditures as a percent of gross national product with that of other countries. On the one hand, this percentage is less than half that of most European countries, but on the other hand, it is not much lower than the percentage in the United States (Table 6-11). Comparing these percentages with the actual dollar equivalents spent per person (shown

Table 6-11. Japan spends almost as large a percentage of her gross national product on social security as does the United States

Country	Social Security as % of GNP	
	1955-56	1968
Japan	4.9	6.0
United States	4.9	7.3
U.S.S.R.	8.0	11.1 (1966-67)
Great Britain	9.6	12.7
France	13.5	15.6 (1965-66)
Italy	10.2	16.2 (1966-67)
West Germany	14.3	17.5

Source: International Labor Office, 1972.

in Table 6-10), and the GNP per capita (shown in Table 2-1), it appears that the United States has such a large GNP per capita that a relatively low percentage of the U. S. GNP spent on social security turns out to be a large absolute amount per person; in contrast, almost the same percentage of GNP spent on social security by Japan turns out to be a small amount per person. Thus, it will be necessary for Japan to increase drastically the percentage of her GNP spent on social security in order even to approach the amounts spent per person by other industrialized countries.

Most informed Japanese appear to be aware that the incomes of many or most older Japanese are low by any standard. Better pensions and higher benefit levels are usually at the top of the list of demands by labor unions, organizations of older Japanese, and other reformers seeking to improve the conditons of the aged. In a survey of Japanese over age 50, which asked, "What policies are essential for the aged?", the most frequent response (63%) was "increased pensions" (Office of the Prime Minister, 1973). In fact, a series of new laws and programs have been put into effect during the last decade which have substantially improved coverage and benefits. Moreover, there is some evidence that these reforms are already improving the income of older Japanese. For example, a survey in 1963 found that three-fourths of the older Japanese were not subject to the resident's tax because they earned less than $500 (Office of the Prime Minister, 1967). Although recent figures exactly comparable have not been found, the data in several tables in this chapter suggest that the majority of older Japanese in 1973 had incomes well above $500 per year. Income for the majority of older Japanese is still low and inadequate, but it is improving substantially.

SUMMARY

The old system of primogeniture provided a kind of "social security" for older Japanese through support by the oldest son. This system was modified after World War II so that inheritances tend to be more evenly distributed among all the children. Along with this change has come increasing belief that pensions or social security, rather than the children, should be primarily responsible for the support of older persons. However, most Japanese with parents still say they would provide support for their parents if they needed it. The actual support patterns show a trend away from family support and toward sufficient income. Nevertheless, at the present time about two-thirds of older Japanese do not have enough income to be self-sufficient. Women, those over 70, and those in rural areas have even less adequate incomes.

The low income of older Japanese appears to be mainly due to the present low pension and social security benefits. All Japanese are covered by some pension program, but most persons now over 65 qualify for only token benefits that provide only "pocket money." Japan spends much less on social security benefits per person over 65 than other industrialized nations. However, as the new pension systems mature, more Japanese will become eligible for more adequate benefits. The income of older Japanese is the gloomiest part of their present picture, but it is beginning to brighten.

7
Respect
for the
Elders

Oyakoko[1] you
do; but do you believe that
grey is beautiful?

If the financial situation of older Japanese is the bleakest part of their picture, the respect and affection they continue to enjoy may be the brightest part. Chapter 2 described the traditional basis of respect for elders, both in the vertical society and in religious doctrines of filial piety. This chapter describes the practices and attitudes that reflect respect for the elders and discusses the extent to which these are changing or persisting.

Respect and affection are difficult concepts to measure, even within one culture. Comparable cross-cultural statistics on respect for the aged are non-existent. Therefore, this chapter contains no tables of statistics, although it refers to some pilot studies which my students conducted in Japan. We can describe only practices and typical attitudes and give our impressions about how widespread they are and how they are changing.

[1]*Oyakoko* is filial duty to parents.

FAMILY RESPECT

We have already described how most older Japanese continue to live with their children; how most of these arrangements appear to be motivated more by desire for companionship, for mutual aid, and attitudes that it is "natural," than by the housing shortage or financial necessity; and how the aged perform many valued services in the household (Chapter 4). We believe this is indirect evidence of a continuing high level of respect and affection for the elders by their families.

Perhaps the most pervasive form of respect for elders in the family (as well as outside the family) is the honorific language used in speaking to or about the elders. English and other languages have polite and impolite forms for some words, but Japanese is unusual in its extreme elaboration of different forms to show the proper degree of respect or deference. Differential respect is reflected not only in the different nouns, verbs, prefixes, suffixes, and other parts of speech, but also in the basic grammar and syntax of the language. There are three basic forms of speech in Japanese: the honorific form, which is used in speaking to or referring to someone who is older or otherwise socially superior to the speaker; the middle form, which is used in speaking to someone on approximately the same social level; and the plain or blunt form, which is usually used in speaking to younger persons and others socially inferior to the speaker. There are many other complications, depending on whether the speaker and listener and person referred to are in the same or different "in-group" or whether the setting is formal or informal, etc. Nevertheless, respect for elders is one of the basic dimensions built into the Japanese language. This is one of the main reasons why it is so difficult for foreigners to learn to speak proper Japanese: not only must they learn the many different forms, but they also must understand the culture enough to know which relationships call for which form.

Another traditional form of respect for elder family members is seating arrangement. The main room of a Japanese house, which usually doubles as a dining-living room during the day and a bedroom at night, contains a *tokonoma*, an alcove in which various scrolls, art objects, or flower arrangements are displayed, depending on the season or occasion. The seat nearest the *tokonoma* is the seat with the highest honor, and the honor of each seat is ranked by its distance from the *tokonoma*. Traditionally, the seat with the highest honor is occupied by the oldest male in the family. His wife would usually occupy the second highest seat, and all the other household members would be arranged in descending order according to age and sex. In many modern households, if the oldest male has retired from being head of the household, the highest seat will be given to the present head of the household, and the oldest male (retired) will be moved down to the second or third highest seat.

The same order of prestige is followed in serving: The oldest male is usually served first; the youngest female is served last. An exception is made for an infant who is usually not made to wait as long as others who are actually higher in status. This custom is reflected in an old term that used to be applied to a second son, "Master Cold-Rice" (*Hiameshi-san*), because the rice may be cooled by the time both his elders and the infants have been served (Hearn, 1955). Not only are the elders served first, they also get the choicest portions of whatever is served.

A similar order of precedence is usually followed in all household matters. The elders and head of household go through doors before younger persons and walk down the street in front of younger persons. The elders and head of household also get to use the family bath (*ofuro*) first. The advantage of this requires some explanation: The *ofuro* is a deep tub of very hot water in which Japanese soak after rinsing off outside the tub. This same water is used for soaking by every one bathing during one evening. Therefore, each person soaking in the *ofuro* leaves a residue of body oils, perspiration, etc., which gradually reduces the purity of the water. Thus the first user gets the cleanest water.

In cooking, also, the tastes of the elders are often given precedence. If the elders like the rice cooked soft for easier chewing, it will usually be cooked soft even if the young want it firm. If the elders like the food salty or sour, it will usually be salty or sour regardless of the other's tastes. The elders and head of household usually get the rooms with the best exposure (usually the sunny one or the one with the best view). They also usually get the best silks, decorations, and bedding (*futon*). When guests bring gifts, the gifts will often be chosen primarily to please the elders.

Adult children who have left the family home show respect and affection for their parents by returning to the family home to celebrate their parents' birthdays and special holidays such as Respect for the Aged Day, *O-bon* festivals, New Year's Day, and Christmas*. Throughout the year dutiful sons and daughters keep in close contact with their parents through frequent visits, letters, and

---

*Christmas is, of course, celebrated in the approximately one percent of homes which are Christian; but a secular version of Christmas is also surprisingly popular in other Japanese homes.

phone calls. (I knew one lady who called her elderly mother by long-distance telephone every day for many years.)

There is a special family celebration to honor the elder when he or she reaches sixty-one years of age. On the sixty-first birthday the elder dons a bright kimono, such as those worn by children, to symbolize that he or she is no longer bound by the somber duties of middleage. Traditionally, all the children and close relatives gather to celebrate this transition. On this day also, or whenever the woman formally retires as mistress of the house, the woman traditionally presents her daughter-in-law with the family rice ladle as the baton of domestic authority. The elder couple then literally retire to a separate room; if possible, a separate retirement cottage may be built for them, and they are referred to as "those living in retirement" (*inkyo*).

In the United States, there is usually little ceremony at family occasions. We often shed even the slight formalities of our etiquette when we come home. In Japan, it is precisely in the family where respect for elders is learned and meticulously observed. Benedict (1946) observed:

While the mother still carries the baby strapped to her back she will push his head down with her hand (to bow), and his first lessons as a toddler are to observe respect behavior to his father or older brother (or grandparents). . . It is no empty gesture. It means that the one who bows acknowledges the right of the other to have his way in things he might well prefer to manage himself, and the one who receives the bow acknowledges in his turn certain responsibilities incumbent upon his station. Hierarchy based on sex and generation and primogeniture are part and parcel of family life (pp. 48f).

When a younger person bows to his elder, the younger person bows lower and stays down longer than the elder. The elder may acknowledge the bow with a simple nod of his head.

There are popular sayings which illustrate family respect for the elders. One riddle says, "Why is a son who wants to offer advice to his parents like a Buddhist priest who wants to have hair on the top of his head?" (Buddhist priests shave their heads.) The answer is, "However much he wants to do it, he can't" (Benedict, 1947). The following dilemma is often posed: If a man's mother and his wife were both drowning at the same time, whom should the man rescue first? In earlier times the answer usually given was his mother because she is elder to his wife. These days the proper answer is not so clear, and there is considerable debate about whether a man's mother or his wife should take precedence. This may be contrasted with the United States where the usual answer would clearly be his wife because a man's primary loyalty is expected to be to his wife.

The reader may notice that we have often used the terms *respect* and *affection* together, and he may question whether these two different attitudes can go together or whether they are mutually incompatible. To contemporary Americans with their strong egalitarian values, it may seem unlikely that one could be truly affectionate toward one before whom he must bow and continually demonstrate his subservience. The Japanese do not usually view this as a problem. In fact, they tend to regard a vertical relationship, with authority and responsibility on one side and respect and subservience on the other, to be conducive to affection between the persons involved. They simply do not value independence and equality in personal relations as much as we do, but rather value dependence and deference in most relationships (Nakane, 1972).

It should be understood that the prerogatives of age are usually balanced by responsibilities and concepts of fairness.

The prerogatives of generation, sex, and age in Japan are great. But those who exercise these privileges act as trustees rather than as arbitrary autocrats. The father or the elder brother is responsible for the household, whether its members are living, dead, or yet unborn. He must make weighty decisions and see that they are carried out. He does not, however, have unconditional authority. He is expected to act responsibly for the honor of the house . . . . The master of the house saddles himself with great difficulties if he acts without regard for group opinion (Benedict, 1946, pp. 54).

Thus, the elder normally "earns" affection and respect from younger family members through his fairness, wisdom, and aid. Hearn describes the ideal traditional Japanese family in utopian terms which show how respect, mutual aid, and affection ideally reinforce one another:

Of course, the old family organization had certain advantages which largely compensated the individual for his state of subjection. It was a society of mutual help; and it was not less powerful to give aid, than to enforce obedience. Every member could do something to assist another member in case of need: each had a right to the protection of all. This remains true of the family today. In a well-conducted household, where every act is performed according to the old forms of courtesy and kindness,—where no harsh word is ever spoken,—where the young look up to the aged with affectionate respect,—where those whom years have incapacitated for more active duty, take upon themselves the care of the children, and render priceless service in teaching and training,—an ideal condition has been realized. The daily life of such a home,—in which the endeavour of each is to make existence as pleasant as possible for all,—in which the bond of union is really love and gratitude,—represents religion in the best and purest sense; and the place is holy . . . (Hearn, 1955, pp. 76).

It seems unlikely that such a utopian household was ever widespread, but the mere existence of such an ideal illustrates the power of respect and affection for elders as motivating forces in Japanese family life.

The question remains: How widespread is such family respect for elders in contemporary Japan? Our interviews with Japanese of all ages in rural and urban areas found estimates ranging from 90 percent in rural areas to a small minority among young urban people. It is safe to say that there is more respect for elders in rural areas, traditional occupations, and households, and among middle-age or older persons than in urban areas, "modern" households, and younger persons. This can also be inferred from the statistics we have presented showing differences by place of residence and age as to living arrangements and support patterns.

An even more difficult question is: How fast are these practices and attitudes changing? It is clear that Western culture and industrialization have made an impact. Older persons who are upset with the decline in respect for elders often blame it on the impact of American occupation after World War II. But because no one has measured the amount of respect for elders either before or after World War II, no one really knows how much impact there was nor how much this respect is changing. My impression is that there has indeed been a substantial change since World War II, so that many of these practices and attitudes of respect have markedly declined, especially among young urban people.

However, there still remain vast differences between the Japanese and Americans in this regard. It is probably true that most Japanese have modified the more extreme expressions of subservience toward elders. Whereas all elders used to be respected simply because they were older, now the majority of elders continues to "earn" respect, but some elders are no longer respected if they are viewed as unjust, immoral, or just unpleasant. In contrast, in America the majority of the aged probably suffer from disrespect simply because they are old (or old-fasioned), and only a minority can maintain much respect from younger generations because of unusual accomplishments and contributions.

PUBLIC RESPECT

The amount of public respect in Japan for elders may be best documented by quoting from the 1963 National Law for the Welfare of the Elders (Number 133):

> The elders shall be loved and respected as those who have for many years contributed toward the development of society, and a wholesome and peaceful life shall be guaranteed to them. In accordance with their desire and ability, the elders shall be given opportunities to engage in suitable work or to participate in social activities.

This law also declares that "any person who is engaged in an enterprise which directly affects the life of the elders shall endeavor to promote the welfare of the elders in the management of that enterprise." Also, "the Central Government and local public bodies have responsibility to promote the welfare of the elders" (Article 4).

In contrast, the comparable law in the United States, the Older Americans' Act of 1965 (US Public Law 89-73), does not make any mention of love and respect for the aged. Nor does it even attempt to *guarantee* a "wholesome and peaceful life." Rather it states only that the duty of the government is to *assist* older people to secure equal opportunity to adequate income, health, housing, employment, etc. (Title 1). This does seem to reflect a basically different attitude toward older people in Japan and the United States.

In order to fulfill its "guarantee" of a wholesome and peaceful life, the Japanese government has undertaken a series of programs for its elders:

1. *Health Examination.* Cities and towns hold annual health examinations for those who are 65 years of age or older. Individual guidance is then given to those who need further diagnosis or treatment.

2. *Home for the Aged.* For those 65 years or older who need to find a protective environment other than their home, the following three kinds of institutions are provided by the law . . . Nursing home (*Yogo Rojin*); Special Nursing Home (*Tokubetsu Yogo Rojin*) for those who are in need of constant medical supervision; and Home with Moderate Fee (*Keihi Rojin*) for those who choose to live in the institution and are able to afford a moderate charge.

3. *Family Foster Care.* For those who have no family to live with.

4. *Grant of Medical Cost.* Free medical care for most persons over age 70.

5. *Home Helper.* Housekeeping help for old people living alone.

6. *Welfare Center for the Aged.* To provide various education, recreational, and consultation services. In 1971 there were 223 such centers.

7. *Other Programs:* including free "gadget-beds" for the bedfast, free employment service, home nurses, telephone centers to provide counseling service to the poor and the lonely, subsidies for sports meetings for the aged, and designation of September 15 as Respect for Elders Day (Ministry of Health and Welfare, 1972, pp. 13f).

Respect for Elders Day (*Keiro No Hi*) is one of the most dramatic expressions of respect and affection for the elders. Ceremonies in honor of the elders have been widespread for more than 300 years, but in 1963 Respect for Elders Day became a national holiday. The law specifies that "the governments of various levels should hold suitable activities to evoke the people's interest in and understanding of the welfare needs of the aged as well as to encourage old people to improve and enrich their own lives." On each September 15 the Health and Welfare Ministry presents a silver cup and a letter from the Premier congratulating each person who reached the age of 100 during the past year. In Tokyo the Metropolitan Government presents a silver fan to those who became 100 during the year; a "respect for elders" medal to those who became 75; and gifts of 5000 yen (about $17) to each of the more than 185,000 persons over the age of 75 in the city. Newspapers run feature articles on the aged and on the celebrations and rallies that are held in most cities. Even small hamlets usually have some kind of ceremony and celebration with gifts of honor for the elders in the community.

During the 1973 Respect for Elders Day, I was able to attend two celebrations in Tokyo. One was sponsored by the Tokyo Metropolitan Government and was held in the dignified Tokyo Public Theatre. Each of the 4000 or so people in the audience was given a Japanese boxed lunch (*bento*) and a souvenir box of rice cakes. The program included a concert by an orchestra, Japanese folk dances, an address by the Emperor's son, the head of the Department of Health and Welfare, and other officials. One theme expressed was that everyone should think of the problems of the aged as his own problem because everyone becomes old. The ceremonies also honored the oldest person in Tokyo (109 years of age) and many leaders of volunteer groups working with the elderly.

The other meeting was sponsored by various unions and was held in the Tokyo Metropolitan Gymnasium. It was filled with about 10,000 people. In addition to entertainment by music and a comedian, the speakers and huge banners demanded: free medical care for all over 65 (not just those over 70); more employment with better pay for the aged; more government money in programs for the aged; and increase in pensions and social security. One speaker asserted, "The problems of the old are problems for everyone. When the problems of the old are solved, everyone will be happy."

A more traditional form of respect for the aged was the practice of younger persons giving their seats to the elders

on public vehicles such as buses, subways, and trains. Traditionally all younger persons were supposed to give their seats to any older person when there were no other seats, simply to show their respect, regardless of whether they appeared infirm or not. In recent years, there have been many complaints, especially from older persons, that younger people are no longer giving their seats to their elders.

As a result, starting on Respect for the Elders Day in 1973 the Central Line (*Chuo Sen*) of the Japanese National Railways, which serves Tokyo and its western suburbs, reserved six seats on every fourth car for use by the aged and the physically handicapped. The seats are silver-grey in color (instead of the usual blue) and are called "silver seats." Prominent signs on the outside and inside of the cars explain that the aged and physically handicapped have priority in the use of these seats. Nevertheless, it appeared to the casual observer that few of these seats were ever used by the aged or physically handicapped.

In order to investigate the extent to which younger people gave up their seats to the aged and specifically how often the silver seats were occupied by the aged, eleven of my students undertook a survey of trains and subways in and around Tokyo. They followed two procedures. First, they observed a series of older persons boarding a train with all the seats filled and counted how many of the older persons were offered seats. These proportions ranged from 10 percent to 73 percent, with an average of 39 percent being offered seats. In Kyoto, which is a more "traditional" city than Tokyo, I observed that most older people were offered seats on the streetcars. Thus, it appears that in modern Tokyo older persons are offered seats somewhat less than half the time, but in more traditional cities, such as Kyoto, most of the elderly are offered seats. By contrast, on the New York City subways and trains, one can assume that older persons are rarely given seats by younger persons.

The second procedure was to count systematically the number of silver seats occupied by the elderly and by younger persons. The proportions occupied by the elderly ranged from 13 percent to 40 percent with an average proportion of 24 percent. Thus, less than a fourth of the silver seats, supposedly reserved for the aged and handicapped, were actually used by the aged. (There were very few used by younger handicapped persons.) One student made a project of observing what happened when older persons got on a car with silver seats which were occupied by younger persons. He found that, in about three-fourths of the cases, the older people just stood in front of the silver seats and the younger people did not offer to give up their seats. In only one-fourth of the cases did the younger person give up his seat, and occasionally this occurred only after the older person pointed out the sign and asked the younger person to get up. Thus, the plan to reserve seats for the aged seems to have failed in its purpose more often than it has succeeded. It is true that this survey was carried out only two months after the plan had been inaugurated, and part of the explanation for its low rate of success could be that many people were still unaware of it. Perhaps with greater familiarity it will become more successful. Most Japanese do tend to abide by most laws and regulations if they are aware of them.

One indirect indicator of rising concern for the elders is the recent growth in gerontology. In the past ten or fifteen years Japan, like the United States and several other industrialized countries, has had a rapid increase in the number of scientists and other professionals doing research and education in gerontology. There are two aspects of this growth, however, that show unusual strength in Japan. One is the fact that the Japanese government now does an annual survey of some aspect of the aged and their problems. Another is the impressive size and resources of the Tokyo Metropolitan Institute on Gerontology. Begun in 1971, this institute in 1973 already had a staff of 174 full-time professionals plus another 100 part-time staff members. It is devoted entirely to research, although the part-time staff usually engages in treatment also. It is housed in a large modern building adjoining several other facilities for the aged including a geriatric hospital, a special nursing home, and apartments for the aged. The Institute contains departments of biology, pathology, biochemistry, pharmacology, physiology, nutrition, psychology, psychiatry, sociology, epidemiology, rehabilitation research, and nursing. It also has special laboratories for electronic microscopy, radioisotopes, computer science, and animals. This institute is much larger and more comprehensive in its research than any institute of gerontology in the United States.

One final and key difference in the attitudes of Japanese and Americans toward aging: most Japanese over 60 do not try to hide their age. In fact, they are usually proud of it. It is considered polite and proper to ask an older Japanese his age and to congratulate him on it. Most Americans know it is impolite to ask an older American his age, and if the truth comes out, the best one can do is to reassure the older person that he does not look or act "that old." I have collected over 30 jokes about older Americans concealing their age (Palmore, 1971). The popularity of hair dyes and cosmetics to conceal wrinkles attest to the prevalence of age concealment among older Americans. Some middle-aged Japanese also dye their greying hair, but most older Japanese do not. It is probably not an exaggeration to say that most Japanese believe "grey is beautiful" and that most Americans do not.

OBASUTE VERSUS RESPECT FOR ELDERS

Ninety miles west of Tokyo there are a railway station and a nearby mountain that bear the name *Obasute*, which means "discarding grandmother." There is no evidence that, at any time in more than a thousand years of recorded history, the Japanese have abandoned the aged as a matter of custom. But the *Obasute* theme can be traced through tales dating from the sixth century to the present (Plath, 1972). The usual theme is set in a mountain village where food is always scarce. Custom in this village decrees that old people make a "pilgrimage" to the mountain during their seventieth year, where they stay and await death. The younger kinsman who accompanies them either abandons them or, if they prove recalcitrant, pushes them over a cliff. The story also can end in three other ways: the younger companion suffers remorse and returns to rescue the old woman; or he returns too late and she is already dead; or the son refuses to abandon his aged mother and hides her away instead. In this latter version, the son is able to solve a series of vexing problems for the ruler of the land, by consulting his hidden parent. As a reward, the ruler offers anything in his power, but the son asks only that the custom of abandonment be abolished (Keene, 1957).

Resentment against the aged is also the main theme of a widely read short story, "The Hateful Age" (*Iyagarase No Nenrei*), by Niwa Fumio (1962). The story is about Old Ume who has been a widow for 54 years and has already out-lived her own children. Her grandchildren feel obligated to care for her, but keep passing her from one to the other. She is withered, feeble, useless, and insensitive:

> Ume had become just a body, in which it was impossible to detect the slightest trace of soul, spirit, conscience, or anything that makes human beings worthy of respect. Her greatest worry in life was that her grand-children or great-grandchildren might be getting better food than she, herself. . . (Such persons) become distasteful, useless lumps of flesh, the scourge of relatives and a burden to society (pp. 340).

A recent best-selling novel, *A Man in a Trance (Kokitsu No Hito)* by Sawako Ariyoshi (1972), depicts the resent-ment against an 84-year-old widower by his son and fami-ly. The widower is senile, and his daughter-in-law hated the fact that she had to take care of him. She often wished for his quick death because she was working, and unex-pected events made it difficult to carry on her work. How-ever, after an incident, her way of thinking changes and she decides to take care of her father-in-law willingly "un-til the end."

These popular stories indicate that there is widespread resentment against the burdens of caring for those few aged who are completely senile and incapacitated. On the other hand, there are many stories which show respect for the elders by portraying them as wise, skillful, and de-voted. The following are some examples of this type.

In the classic story, "Robe of Feathers," it is the aged Mother who wisely advises her son not to try to keep an angel captive: "My son, it is not wise to meddle in the af-fairs of these unearthly people." But the son loves the angel so much that he does keep her captive and, as a result, the angel's beauty slowly dims until one day she escapes and leaves the son heartbroken (Harris, 1937).

Another classic story, with some historical basis, is about Okubo Hikozayemon who is described as a "brusque, humorous, self-willed old fellow." The Shogun Iyeyasu (sixteenth century) grew to love him "almost as a brother" because of his blunt honesty and loyalty. When he was offered the position of *Daimyo,* or lord, he refused, but instead asked permission of the *Shogun* to do anything he wished such as being insolent and critical to the lords and even to the Shogun himself. The *Shogun* agreed and as a result, "If any *Daimyo* should lose his loyalty to that line, was too extravagant, or fail in any other way, Hikozayemon would be there to chastise him without fear or mercy." Hikozayemon even tore the branches off the *Shogun's* prize Kimura Plum Tree to show the *Shogun* how cruel was his rule that punished by death anyone who broke a branch of the tree. The Shogun realized the foolishness of his rule and confessed, "Truly, I was wrong, old man, and you were right." The story concludes:

This licensed insolence of Okubo Hikozayemon often tasted as a bitter medicine to others, but it was a tonic medicine, and helped to preserve the peace and power of those three successive Shoguns to the end of his own long life (Harris, 1936, pp. 224f).

A modern story titled "Saigo Takamori" is about a wise old professor who meets a know-it-all student on a train and challenges his absolute faith in historical records by making him think that Saigo Takamori (a famous General who was supposed to have committed suicide in 1877) may still be alive (Akutagawa, 1964). The wisdom and skill of the elders are also illustrated by the modern story of Takizawa Bakin, an elderly author who is still an inspired and sensitive master-writer (Akutagawa, 1964).

Respect for the authority of the elders is illustrated by

"Morning Mist" which involves an old professor of mathematics and his son who wants to get married. The old father is reluctant to give permission to his son to marry because he does not want a new person in the household who might upset his routine. Despite the fact that the old father is getting senile and obsessive about routine and order, his authority to withhold permission is never questioned (Tatsuo, 1962).

My observations and interviews in Japan convinced me that these positive images of the elders are more common than the negative images shown in the *"Obasute* theme" stories. Certainly, the vast majority of Japanese still have substantially more respect and affection for most of their elders than do most Americans.

Ruth Benedict contrasts our attitudes with the Japanese attitudes by describing two different "arcs of life":

The arc of life in Japan is plotted in opposite fashion to that in the United States. It is a great shallow U-curve with maximum freedom and indulgence allowed to babies and to the old. Restrictions are slowly increased after babyhood till having one's own way reaches a low just before and after marriage. This low line continues many years during the prime of life, but the arc gradually ascends again until after the age of sixty men and women are almost as unhampered by shame as little children are. In the United States we stand this curve upside down. Firm disciplines are directed toward the infant and these are gradually relaxed as the child grows in strength until a man runs his own life when he gets a self-supporting job and when he sets up a household of his own. The prime of life is with us—the high point of freedom and initiative. Restrictions begin to appear as men lose their grip or their energy or become dependent. It is difficult for Americans even to fantasy a life arranged according to the Japanese pattern (1946, pp. 254).

This contrast has probably lessened since World War II, with the Japanese becoming somewhat more like Americans, and of course there are always exceptions to such simplified patterns. Nevertheless, the contrast provides a

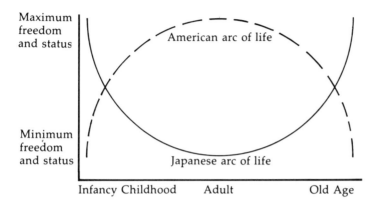

Figure 7-1. *Japanese and American Arc of Life* (after Benedict, 1946)

graphic way to visualize basic differences in life cycles (see Figure 7-1).

A way to visualize the change in respect and status of the aged in Japan and the United States is presented in Figure 7-2. There is considerable evidence that the status of the aged in the United States has been declining, at least since the turn of the century. Equality Indexes comparing

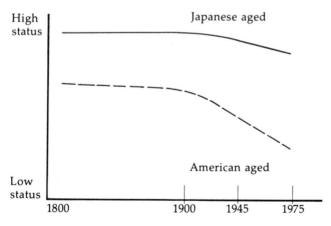

Figure 7-2. *Change in respect and status of Japanese and American aged*

aged with non-aged Americans in the areas of income, weeks worked, hours worked, industry and education all show substantial declines since 1940 (Palmore and Whittington, 1971). In contrast, Equality Indexes in Japan show relatively little decline (Chapter 5). Thus, Figure 7-2 shows a marked decline in the status of American aged beginning at about the turn of the century, while there is relatively little decline shown for the status of the Japanese aged and it begins mainly after World War II. This is only a theoretical graph because we do not have sufficient data to plot precisely either the relative levels or the amount of change. However, the evidence we do have supports the general pattern shown.

Indeed, there is some evidence that there may be a resurgence of respect for the elders in Japan. In recent years there has been a resurgence of many traditional Japanese practices ranging from the greater use of traditional Japanese dress to exhortations for more filial piety. For example, the city of Atsugi in Kanagawa Prefecture recently declared itself the "City of Filial Piety" and adopted a charter extolling the virtue of filial piety (*Japan Times*, 1974). This may be a sign that respect for the elders is beginning to move toward pre-war levels.

SUMMARY

Traditional practices in the family which show respect for the elders include honorific language, giving the best seats to the elders, serving elders first, elders going through doors first, using the bath first, catering to the tastes of elders in cooking, children returning to parents' home for holidays and birthdays, the special celebration of the sixty-first birthday, and bowing to elders. Family respect for elders is also reflected in several popular sayings. Respect for elders is usually accompanied by affection based on the elders' fairness, wisdom and aid. Respect for elders is more widespread in rural areas than urban, more in traditional households than modern, and more among the middle-aged than among the younger children. Patterns of respect appear to be changing, especially since World War II, so that the more extreme forms of subservience are declining, and some elders are no longer respected if they are viewed as unjust, immoral, or unpleasant.

Public respect for elders is demonstrated by the National Law for Welfare of the Aged, Respect for Elders Day, and the practice of younger persons giving their seats to elders on public vehicles. Our survey found that younger persons gave their seats to elders about two-fifths of the time in Tokyo, but most of the time in Kyoto. A new regulation reserving some seats for the elders on commuting trains in Tokyo appeared to work about one-fourth of the time. The growth of gerontology and the impressive size and resources of the Tokyo Metropolitan Institute on Gerontology reflect the growing concern in Japan for the problems of the aged.

In contrast to the traditional respect for elders, there is also a theme of resentment and desire to abandon senile and incapacitated aged which can be found in many stories and a recent best-selling novel. Nevertheless, there are still basic differences between Japan and the United States in attitudes and treatment of the aged. These differences are illustrated by Benedict's "Arc of Life" and by a graph showing earlier and greater decline of respect for the aged in American than for the elders in Japan. In short, most Japanese think "grey is beautiful;" most Americans do not.

8
Activities and Satisfaction

Morning, noon, and night,
actions and satisfactions,
chicken and the egg.

We have shown how the Japanese elders are more integrated and active in their families and in the labor force. This chapter focuses on their other activities and what satisfactions they derive from these activities, as well as their dissatisfactions and fears about the future. Finally, it discusses some evidence relevant to the activity versus disengagement controversy.

ACTIVITIES

What do the honorable elders do with their time? How many hours do they spend in sleep, in obligated duties, and how many hours of leisure time remain? They appear to sleep about the same number of hours as older Americans, but because of more time spent at work and doing housework, older Japanese have about one-third less leisure time (Table 8-1). This fits the general pattern of greater activity and involvement among older Japanese.

As in other industrialized countries, the most frequent leisure activity of the elders is watching television and list-

Table 8-1. Older Japanese have less leisure time than older Americans

| Age Groups | Average Hours per Day | | | |
	Sleep	Obligated Time	Leisure Time	Total
Japanese aged 60+	8.8	9.6	5.6	24.0
Americans aged 65+	9.0	6.7	8.4	24.0

Source: Japan—Ministry of Health and Welfare, 1972; America—Beyer and Woods, 1963. (The American survey was of Social Security Beneficiaries. If non-beneficiaries had been included, leisure time would have been somewhat less.)

ening to the radio. Among men, the next most frequent leisure activities are reading and gardening. Among women, the next most frequent activities are those in the crafts and arts (Table 8-2).

About half the elders have hobbies such as gardening and *bonsai* (the growing and shaping of miniature trees), flower arranging, tea ceremony, travel (mainly to shrines and scenic spots), playing *go* and *shogi* (the Japanese equivalents of checkers and chess), playing instruments such as the *Samisen*, singing, sports, folk dance, drawing and

Table 8-2. Most frequent leisure activities of Japanese over 60 (percent who regularly engage in the activity)

Activity	Total	Men	Women
Television, radio	78	80	71
Reading	30	40	20
Gardening	29	37	21
Crafts & arts	21	2	40
Visiting	21	22	20
Walking	16	20	12
Club activities	16	17	15
Other leisure activities	18	20	17

Source: *Welfare Journal,* 1971.

calligraphy (the art of drawing Japanese characters for wall hangings) (*Welfare Journal*, 1971). We do not have exactly comparable data on how many older Americans have hobbies, but one national survey found that less than 20 percent of Americans over 60 regularly engage in hobby activities, even when they are broadly defined to include sports, music, and indoor games such as chess and checkers (*Opinion Research Corporation*, 1957, pp. A-63). Thus, it may be that, despite having less leisure time, more older Japanese have hobbies than older Americans.

Another frequent activity of Japanese elders is visiting with their neighbors. A majority say they "often" visit neighbors, and another third say they "occasionally" visit (Table 8-3). There is apparently more visiting done in rural areas with only 8 percent saying they do not visit neighbors. This fits with the data given earlier (Chapter 4) showing that few older Japanese report being lonely.

Going on overnight trips to visit shrines, scenic spots, and relatives is another favorite activity of the majority of elders, especially among those aged 60 to 70 (Ministry of Health and Welfare, 1972). The majority of those going on overnight trips, do so several times each year. Typically these trips are taken with friends or family members, but

Table 8-3. A majority of older Japanese often visit with neighbors (percentage distribution)

Visits	Total	Big Cities	Other Cities	Rural
Often visit neighbors	55	36	51	65
Occasionally visit	32	44	34	27
No visits	12	19	14	8
No answer	1	1	1	1
Total	100	100	100	100

Source: *Welfare Journal*, 1971.

going with a club, with fellow workers, or on commercial tours are also frequent. Only 5 percent make such trips alone. It is a common sight in Japan to see groups of a dozen or so grey-haired elders being led around by a tour guide with a flag at the head of the column.

We have mentioned how most cities and towns have special clubs for the elders which are usually organized and subsidized by the government. One survey found that one third of all Japanese over age 65 belong to these clubs (National Life Center, 1972). Participation is greater in rural areas and among those over 70 (Table 8-4). These clubs usually meet at least once a month for lectures, gardening and landscaping the community, cleaning and repairing community centers, singing and dancing parties, going to an *onsen* (public hot bath) party, study meetings, etc. These clubs also occasionally participate in the demonstrations held to demand more government aid for the problems of the aged. Thus, the elders' clubs serve

Table 8-4. A third of older Japanese participate in clubs for elders (percentage distribution)

Groups	Know About Clubs	Participate	Not Participate	Don't Know About Clubs
Total 60+	80	31	49	20
By size:				
Large cities	67	15	51	33
Other cities over 100,000	79	29	51	21
Cities less than 100,000	80	30	51	20
Rural areas	85	43	43	15
By age:				
60-64	81	18	63	19
65-69	80	32	48	20
70+	79	44	35	21

Source: National Life Center, 1972.

multiple functions: community service, study and action aimed at helping elders, group recreation, group identification, and mutual support among the elders.

SATISFACTIONS AND DISSATISFACTIONS

What activities are most frequently satisfying? The older men most often say job-related activities are most satisfying, while the older women say family activities are most satisfying (Table 8-5). This shows a continuation among the elders of the tradition that a woman's place in in the home, and a man's place is the world of work. However, another survey found that in the seventies there is a decrease in both job satisfactions and family activity satisfactions, with a corresponding increase in the proportions who do not mention any satisfying activities (an increase from about one-third to about one-half; National Life Center, 1972).

A good comparison between the overall satisfaction of Japanese and American aged is possible with statistics from an international survey which used the Cantril "Sat-

Table 8-5. Job activities are more frequently satisfying to men; family activities, to women (percentage distribution)

	"What satisfying activities do you have?"	
Activities	*Men over 60*	*Women over 60*
Job	34	13
Family	28	36
Hobbies	16	14
Social	4	4
No answer	26	32

Source: Office of Prime Minister, 1973. (Totals add to more than 100 percent because of some multiple answers.)

isfaction Ladder" (Cantril, 1965). In this survey persons of all ages were asked to imagine the best possible and the worst possible life for them, and then to rate themselves on a satisfaction ladder with zero representing the worst possible and 10 representing the best possible life. They did this three times: for the present time, for five years ago, and for five years in the future. The results show that, for both Japan and the United States, those over 65 ranked themselves at present about the same as the younger people in their country (Table 8-6). However the older Japanese show a pattern of substantial *increases* in satisfaction from the past to the present to the future, whereas older Americans show a decline in satisfaction from the past to the present and almost no change from the present to the future. This difference cannot be explained by the tendency of all Japanese to show increased satisfaction from past to future, because all Americans, except for the aged, show an even greater tendency to show increased satisfaction from past to future. This difference in patterns apparently means that although older Americans tend to see their satisfactions as decreasing from the past to the present and future, older Japanese tend to see their satisfactions as increasing both in the present and in the future.

Table 8-6. Satisfaction ratings for Japan and the United States (mean personal satisfaction ladder ratings)

Age Groups	Past	Present	Future
All Japanese over 21	4.6	5.2	6.2
Japanese over 65	4.9	5.2	5.9
All Americans over 21	5.9	6.6	7.8
Americans over 65	6.9	6.5	6.6

Source: Cantril, 1965.

This difference in patterns is what one would expect from the greater integration and respect for the elders in Japan. Its implication for the activity versus disengagement controversy will be discussed in the next section.

A similar difference between the aged in Japan and in the United States is found when surveys of dissatisfaction and worry are compared. Only small proportions of Japanese over 60 years of age report disatisfactions in the areas of health, housing, finances, employment, etc., whereas half or more of Americans over 60 report worry about making ends meet, money in old age, and health (Tables 8-7 and 8-8). Also, substantial proportions of older Americans are worried about a good place to live and about keeping their jobs. It is also significant that the most frequently reported dissatisfaction in Japan was with the person's own health, about which little can be done in most cases. Things that could be changed by different national policy or action of the community or family, such as housing, finances, and family relations, resulted in only 5 percent or less reporting dissatisfactions.

Table 8-7. Small proportions of older Japanese report dissatisfactions (percentage distribution by age groups)

Dissatisfaction	Total 60+	60-69	70-79	80+
Health	16	13	18	19
Housing	5	6	4	2
Financial	4	4	3	4
Physical environment	4	6	3	3
Family relations	4	3	5	3
Employment	2	3	2	—
Relations with neighbors	1	1	—	1
No special dissatisfaction	59	61	60	57
No answer, don't know	6	5	5	13
Total	100	100	100	100

Source: National Life Center, 1972.

Table 8-8. A majority of older Americans worry about various things (percentage distribution of persons 60+)

Type of Worry	Worry a Lot	Worry Sometimes	Do Not Worry	Total
Making ends meet	21	37	42	100
Money in old age	22	27	51	100
Health	15	35	50	100
A good place to live	8	22	70	100
Keeping your job	5	16	79	100

Source: Bock and Gergen, 1966.

Lastly, it is only health dissatisfactions which increase with age: all the others stay about the same or go down in the older age categories. This seems to indicate that as the Japanese elders get older, they tend to become more satisfied with life, except for their health. This can be contrasted with a survey of Americans over 60 which found that morale tended to decline in the older age categories (Kutner, 1956).

With the changes that are occurring in the situation of Japanese elders, what is their view of the future? A majority did not report any specific fears about the future, but there was more widespread fear reported in the large cities (with the exception of Tokyo) than in small cities and rural areas (Table 8-9). This may reflect the greater decline in respect for the elders and in the integration of the elders in the metropolitan areas than in other areas. It is surprising to find less fear in Tokyo than in other cities. This may reflect a greater emphasis on programs and services for the elders in Tokyo than in other cities. The Governor of Tokyo, Dr. Ryokichi Minobe, has a special interest in problems of the elders and has been pushing special programs for the elders since 1968. The unique Tokyo

Table 8-9. More of the older Japanese in large cities (except Tokyo) have fears about the future.

	Percent
Total aged 50+	42
Area:	
Tokyo	37
9 large cities	51
Other cities of 100,000+	45
Cities of less than 100,000	36
Rural areas	40

Source: Office of Prime Minister, 1973

Metropolitan Institute of Gerontology (described in Chapter 7) is one example of these programs.

When younger people are asked about their fears for old age, only a third express any fears, and most of those expressed have to do with income and with health (National Life Center, 1972). These fears appear to be well-based because of the low incomes of older Japanese (discussed in Chapter 6), and because of the well-known tendency toward declining health in old age. It is remarkable that less than 6 percent express any other fears about old age, such as fears about family relations, employment, and housing.

Table 8-10. Fears about old age are increasing among Japanese (percentage distribution of persons aged 20+)

Answer	1960	1964	1971
Sometimes have fears about old age	28	28	36
Don't have fears about old age	72	59	58
No answer; don't know		13	6
Total	100	100	100

Source: National Life Center, 1972.

However, fears about old age appear to have increased since 1964. In 1960 and in 1964, 28 percent of persons over age 20 said they sometimes have fears about old age, but by 1971 that proportion had increased to 36 percent (Table 8-10). This is probably due to an increasing recognition of the problems of old age. On the other hand, almost two-thirds still report no worries about old age.

ACTIVITY VERSUS DISENGAGEMENT

As stated in the introductory chapter, one of the two main theories guiding this study of Japanese elders is disengagement theory. The opposing viewpoint is known as activity theory. In order to evaluate the evidence we found, it is necessary to understand the main propositions of these two conflicting theories. Havighurst summarized as follows:

(activity theory) implies that, except for the inevitable changes in biology and in health, older people are the same as middle-aged people, with essentially the same psychological and social needs. In this view, the decreased social interaction that characterizes old age results from the withdrawal by society from the aging person; and the decrease in interaction proceeds against the desires of most aging men and women. The older person who ages optimally is the person who stays active and who manages to resist the shrinkage of his social world. He maintains the activities of middle age as long as possible and then finds substitutes for those activities he is forced to relinquish: substitutes for work when he is forced to retire; substitutes for friends and loved ones whom he loses by death (Havighurst, 1968, pp. 161).

In contrast, the disengagement theory states:

. . . the decreased social interaction is interpreted as a process characterized by mutuality; one in which both society and the aging person withdraw, with the aging individual acceptant, perhaps even desirous of the decreased interaction. It is suggested that the individual's withdrawal has intrinsic, or developmental, qualities; . . . and that, in this sense, disengagement is a natural rather than an imposed process. In this view, the older person who has a sense of psychological well-being will usually be the person who has reached a new equilibrium characterized by a greater psychological distance, altered types of relationships, and decreased social interaction with the persons around him (Havighurst, 1968, pp. 161).

Thus, there are two main points of contention between these theories: (1) Disengagement theory claims that withdrawal of aging persons from activity and involvement is intrinsic, natural, and typical; while activity theory maintains that withdrawal is not intrinsic, natural, or typical, and that when withdrawal occurs it is usually imposed by society in opposition to the natural needs and desires of normal aging persons. (2) Disengagement theory implies that disengagement leads to better health through the conservation of dwindling energy and to better psychological well-being; while activity theory asserts that continued activity and involvement tend to maintain health and life satisfaction. In short, disengagement theory asserts that disengagement is normal, healthy, and satisfying; activity theory asserts that activity is normal, healthy, and satisfying.

Which theory is supported by a comparison of Japan and the United States? First we have seen how the Japanese elders are more active and involved than the older Americans in their families, in work, and in various activities. Second, we have seen that the Japanese elders appear to be as healthy or healthier than older Americans. Third, we have seen that Japanese elders tend to report increasing life satisfaction, while older Americans report decreasing life satisfaction. These three facts support the activity theory that activity is usually healthy and satisfying.

Table 8-11. Those who continue working are healthier (percentage distributions of Japanese over 60)

Health	Working	Not Working
Good	44	23
Average	41	39
Poor	15	38
Total	100	100

Source: Office of the Prime Minister, 1973.

Which theory is supported when we compare the more active with the more disengaged elders in Japan? We find that older Japanese who keep working and older Japanese who favor continued work are healthier (Tables 8-11 and 8-12). We also find that those who like doing voluntary activities are healthier than those who do not like voluntary activities (Table 8-13). Finally, those who continue working and those who like doing voluntary work more often report life satisfaction than those who are not working and those who do not like voluntary activities (Table 8-14). Thus, among the Japanese elders activity is associated with better health and more life satisfaction. The

Table 8-12. Those who favor continued work are healthier (percentage distribution of Japanese over 60).

Attitude	Good Health	Average Health	Poor Health
It is better to work as long as possible	86	74	67
It is better not to work in old age	11	18	22
No answer; don't know	3	8	10
Total	100	100	100

Source: Office of the Prime Minister, 1973.

Table 8-13. Those who like doing volunteer activities are healthier (percentage distributions of Japanese over 60)

Attitude	Good Health	Average Health	Poor Health
Like voluntary activities	46	37	29
Don't like voluntary activities	25	32	37
No answer; don't know	29	31	34
Total	100	100	100

Source: Office of the Prime Minister, 1973.

difficulty with interpreting these facts as supporting activity theory is the old "chicken and egg" problem: which comes first? It may be that better health and satisfaction is what causes greater activity, rather than the other way around. Our interpretation would be that activity, health, and satisfaction are three mutually reinforcing factors: activity promotes better health and satisfaction because activity involves physical exercise, mental stimulation, and social interaction; better health makes possible more activity and is a universal value directly causing more satisfaction; satisfaction stimulates activity while despair and depression lead to inactivity; satisfaction also leads to

Table 8-14. More of those who continue working and who like doing voluntary activities have life satisfaction (percentage distributions of Japanese over 60)

	Working	Not Working	Like Voluntary Activities	Don't Like Voluntary Activities
Have life satisfactions	83	65	84	66
Have no life satisfaction	17	35	16	34
Total	100	100	100	100

Source: Office of the Prime Minister, 1973.

better mental and physical health through various psy-chosomatic mechanisms. Thus, the association of activity, health, and satisfaction among Japanese elders supports activity theory rather than disengagement theory.

SUMMARY

Japanese elders have less leisure time than older Ameri-cans because the Japanese spend more time at work and doing housework. Among the most frequent leisure ac-tivities are watching television, listening to radio, read-ing, gardening (especially among men), crafts and arts (especially among women). About half the elders have hobbies such as gardening, *bonsai*, flower arranging, tea ceremony, travel, and music. Frequent social activities are visiting with neighbors and elders' club activities.

Men most often report job-related activities as most satisfying, whereas women most often report family ac-tivities as most satisfying. The Japanese elders report a rising pattern of life satisfaction from past to present to future, whereas older Americans report decreasing satis-faction from past to present and future. Fewer of the Japa-nese elders report dissatisfactions compared to older Americans and most of the elders' dissatisfactions have to do with poor health. Furthermore, non-health dissatis-factions tend to *decline* with age among the Japanese elders. Although a majority report no specific fears about the future, there are more fears reported in the cities than in rural areas.

Only a third of younger people express any fears about the future, and most of these have to do with health and income. However, there has been some increase in fears since 1964.

Activity theory is supported by a comparison of Japanese elders to older Americans: the Japanese are more active, more satisfied, and as healthy as the Americans. Activity theory is also supported by comparisons of the more active to less active Japanese elders: the more active persons are healthier and more satisfied. We conclude that activity, health, and satisfaction are three mutually reinforcing factors.

9
Conclusions

Autumn years of life
need not decline. They can be
opportunity.

CULTURE CAN MAINTAIN STATUS OF AGED

The first purpose of this study was to examine the status of older Japanese in order to find out whether it has declined with industrialization or has maintained relatively high levels. Most of the evidence indicates that the status of Japanese elders has suffered little decline and is substantially higher than that of the aged in other industrialized countries.

The health status of Japanese elders has been improving with better nutrition, sanitation, and medical care so that they are now about as healthy as the aged in other modern countries. The Japanese elders are much more integrated in their families as shown by their living arrangements and functions in the household. Furthermore, there has been little decline in proportions living with their children so that over two-thirds will probably continue to live with their children during the foreseeable future.

The employment status of the elders is much higher than in other industrialized countries: over half the older men continue to be employed. Most of those who stop work, do so for voluntary and health reasons rather than being forced to stop by compulsory retirement or other discrimination against the aged. The trends indicate little decline in employment status. Those who are not employed do tend to have relatively low independent incomes, but pensions and retirement benefits are rapidly improving, and the system of family support usually assures at least the minimum necessities of life.

The main explanation for their relatively high status and integration is the tradition of respect for elders which has its roots in the vertical society and in religious docdrines of filial piety. Respect and affection for the elders are shown on a daily basis by honorific language; bowing; priority for the elders in seating, serving, bathing, and going through doors. It is also reflected in popular sayings, special celebrations of the sixty-first birthday, the national observance of Respect for Elders Day, and the National Law for Welfare of the Aged.

We therefore conclude that the theory of marked decline in the status of the aged as a necessary result of industrialization is false. On the contrary, Japan shows that a tradition of respect for the aged can maintain their relatively high status and integration despite industrialization.

This conclusion challenges the Marxian theory that culture and social structure are determined by the economic system and that a person's status is determined by his relationship to the means of production. If this theory were applicable to the Japanese elders, the high degree of industrialization in Japan and the elders' lower level of employment (compared to agricultural societies) would cause them to have a low status. On the contrary, their relatively high status supports the Weberian theory that culture can have an independent effect on the economic and social structure, as shown by the effect of the tradition of respect for elders on their status and integration into the family, economy, and community.

How does this conclusion compare to the conclusions

of Cowgill and Holmes' major cross-cultural study, *Aging and Modernization* (1972)? They recognize three exceptions to the theory of low status for the aged in modern societies: Russia, migrants to Israel from Oriental societies, and "possibly" the case of Ireland. I believe Japan should be added to this list of exceptions.

In *Aging and Modernization*, David Plath gives his impressions which emphasize the negative and unhappy aspects of aging in Japan (pp. 133-150). I believe these impressions are one-sided for two reasons: he apparently had access to little of the statistical data such as we have presented, and he tends to emphasize the negative aspects of the data he does present. For example, he interprets the high suicide rate among older Japanese as a symptom of low and unhappy status; a more likely explanation is that Japanese culture tends to produce more suicides at all ages. In another example he quotes one person as estimating that "one in five old people is not effectively included in day-to-day family conversation and activity" (pp. 142). Even assuming this estimate to be accurate (one in ten would probably be more accurate), one could look at the other side and conclude that most of the aged are highly integrated in their families because four out of five are effectively included in day-to-day family conversation and activity. For a third example, he states, "And six per cent of those living with a child openly told interviewers that they would rather be living elsewhere right then—if there were some place to go" (pp. 143). Again, one could turn this around and say that 94 percent of those living with a child reported no desire to live elsewhere. In fairness, Plath admits "I have tended to paint the darker side of aging in Japan" (pp. 150). As a result, his picture is a gloomy distortion of the reality enjoyed by most Japanese elders.

In their final chapter, Cowgill and Holmes list a series of propositions about the relationships between modernization and aging. The evidence from Japan supports nine of those propositions but contradicts or fails to support four of them. The evidence is unclear on three propositions dealing with primitive societies. The supported propositions are:

1. Longevity is directly and significantly related to the degree of modernization.
2. Modernized societies have older populations: i.e., higher proportions of old people.
3. Modern societies have higher proportions of women and especially of widows.
4. Modern societies have higher proportions of people who live to be grandparents and even great grandparents.
5. The status of the aged is high in societies in which there is a high reverence for or worship of ancestors.
6. The status of the aged is high in those societies in which they are able to continue to perform useful and valued functions; however, this is contingent upon the values of the society as well as upon the specific activities of the aged.
7. The status of the aged is high in societies in which the extended form of the family is prevalent and tends to be lower in societies which favor the nuclear form of the family and neolocal marriage.
8. With modernization the responsibility for the provision of economic security for dependent aged tends to be shifted from the family to the state.
9. The individualistic value system of western society tends to reduce the security and status of older people (pp. 322f).

The propositions contradicted or not supported by Japan are:

1. The status of the aged is inversely proportional to the rate of social change. (Japan has experienced one of the fastest rates of social change.)
2. The status of the aged tends to be high in agricultural societies and lower in urbanized societies. (The status of the aged in Japan ap-

pears to be as high or higher than that in many agricultural societies.)

3. The proportion of the aged who are able to maintain leadership roles
   declines with modernization. (Japan appears to have as many aged
   in leadership roles now as before modernization.)

4. . . . an increasing tendency toward disengagement appears to ac-
   company modernization (pp. 322f). (We have shown how Japanese
   aged appear to have maintained their participation in the family,
   work force, and community.)

All the above propositions were derived from the findings of eighteen different investigators in as many different contemporary countries. Nevertheless, the evidence
from Japan contradicts or questions four of the basic
propositions. These four propositions need to be revised
to take into account this new evidence.

ACTIVITY THEORY

The second purpose of this study was to examine the
evidence from Japan bearing on the controversy between
disengagement and activity theory. There are several aspects to these theories and they have been stated with
varying degrees of caution or extremeness. In order to sim-
plify and clarify the points of contention we have focused
on two main questions. Is disengagement intrinsic, natural, and typical or is it imposed by society in opposition
to the natural needs and desires of normal aging persons?
Does disengagement promote better health and life satisfaction or does continued activity promote better health
and satisfaction?

Stated in these simple and extreme forms, it should be
obvious that neither theory will apply to all persons in all
places. Some older people in some cultures typically disengage, and for some of these people health and satisfac-

tion are maintained by their disengagement. Other older people typically maintain high levels of activity, and for some of these people health and satisfaction are maintained by their activity. Specification of the factors which determine whether a person will disengage or remain active and specification of the conditions under which disengagement or activity will be beneficial are the next major areas of research needed in this controversy.

Furthermore, it should be obvious that the *amount* of disengagement or activity can vary enormously and on different levels such as the physical, psychological, and social. Disengagement theorists would not argue that extreme disengagement to the point of no physical activity, no mental activity, and no social interaction is either typical or beneficial. And activity theorists would not argue that frantic physical, mental, or social activity is typical or beneficial. The real question is what level and what mix of activity and disengagement is most typical and most beneficial for different types of older persons. Thus, broad generalizations about unspecified levels of activity are not very useful for a given individual.

But this is true of most broad generalizations, and if the above qualifications and complications are kept in mind, it can be useful on the theoretical level to see which general theory the evidence tends to support.

The comparison of Japanese elders to older Americans found that the Japanese elders are more active and involved, that they are about as healthy, and that they report more increasing satisfaction and less dissatisfactions. Second, comparisons of the more active Japanese elders with the more disengaged found that the more active are healthier and more satisfied. We recognized the "chicken and egg" problem here and interpreted the data as show-them. Americans sometimes use the twenty-first birthday as an occassion to recognize the new adult. Other rites of passage for the young are confirmation or bar mitzvah, graduation, marriage, and christening ceremonies. There are few such ceremonies for older persons. Sometimes a golden wedding anniversary (after 50 years of marriage) becomes an occasion for recognizing and showing affection for older couples. Sometimes retirement parties are held to recognize an employee's contribution. It might also be useful for Americans to observe the sixty-fifth birthday with special celebrations in order to encourage more respect and affection for our elders.

3. In our supposedly egalitarian society, it is unlikely that Americans would adopt forms of deference toward older people such as bowing and honorific language. Nevertheless, we do have a weak tradition of "age before beauty" when going through doors and when serving people. This saying implies that the aged are not beautiful and therefore I believe it should not be perpetuated. However, it may be that strengthening and extending the tradition of precedence for older persons would help restore more respect for elders and more self-respect among older persons themselves.

4. We also have a weak tradition of giving seats to elders on crowded public transportation. This could be reinforced, as the Japanese have done, by regulations which give priority to older persons for a certain number of seats in each bus or train. In addition to recognizing special privileges for elders, this would facilitate the ease of travel of older persons, more of whom must rely exclusively on public transportation.

5. All older Japanese are eligible for a minimum income payment from the government. While this amounts

ing that activity, health, and satisfaction are three mutually reinforcing factors. Therefore, we conclude that the evidence from Japan tends to support activity theory rather than disengagement theory.

SUGGESTIONS

Our third purpose was to find patterns of attitudes and behaviors in Japan which might suggest ways that the West could adopt to improve the situation of its elders. We will proceed from relatively simple ideas to the more complex.

1. Respect for the Elders Day is a popular national holiday and apparently succeeds in encouraging respect for the elders and a greater awareness of their problems, as well as actions to reduce these problems. Labor Day and Veterans Day in the United States are similar national holidays which recognize the contributions of labor and veterans as well as enouraging more recognition of their problems. Mother's Day and Father's Day are not official government holidays, but are widely observed in a variety of ways to recognize the contributions of mothers and fathers. Thus, there seems to be ample precedent for establishing an Older Americans Day in the United States which would be similar in function to Japan's Respect for Elders Day. One difficulty is that while laborers, veterans, mothers, and fathers are generally proud, or at least not ashamed, of their status, many older Americans are ashamed of their status and try to deny their old age. Presumably, if an Older Americans Day could be established, it would help reduce this shame about old age.

2. The Japanese also use the sixty-first birthday as an occasion to honor the elders and to express affection for

to little more than pocket money at present, the principle of a minimum income guaranteed by the government for older persons is a good one. As of January 1974, the United States started a program guaranteeing a minimum income to persons over 65 of $140 per month ($210 for a couple). Thus, we have just adopted the principle of minimum incomes for the aged. The next step would be to raise the level of this minimum from its present poverty level to a more adequate income.

6. Several cities in Japan have established programs in which elders living alone are visited or called on a daily basis in order to see if they are all right or need anything. Such a program in the United States would not only reduce the fears of older persons living alone that they might have some kind of accident or even die before anyone could be reached, but it would also reduce their isolation. There is evidence that isolation can lead to mental and even physical deterioration.

7. It is a widespread practice for Japanese of all ages to begin their day with some kind of group exercise. This is carried over into homes for the aged in which the day typically begins with a combination of group exercise and folk dance in rhythm to music. Such morning exercise is widely recognized as an excellent way to preserve physical and mental functioning. When it is done on a group basis, there is the added satisfaction of social support and interaction. Instituting such programs of exercise for older Americans should improve their physical and mental health.

8. The Japanese government encourages and subsidizes sports days for the elders. Generally, this takes the form of various track and field events which are not too strenuous for healthy older persons. If the U. S. govern-

ment encouraged and subsidized such sports days for older Americans, this too should improve the physical and mental health of those who participate.

9. Another program to improve the health of Japanese elders is the free annual health examination which is followed by more detailed examinations and treatments for those who need it. The present Medicare program for older Americans does not cover such routine examinations. It would seem that with only a modest cost to the program, it could be extended to cover an annual examination in order to detect and prevent the development of many serious diseases.

10. Starting in 1973, the Japanese government began providing completely free medical care to most Japanese over age 70. Some cities provide free medical care to their residents between the ages of 65 and 70. The present Medicare program in the United States covers only about one-half the medical care cost of older Americans. Completely free medical care would remove the high financial barriers that remain between many older Americans and adequate medical care. This would not only improve the health of older Americans and thus improve their life satisfaction directly, but it would also prevent the depletion of financial resources which so often results from the expenses of serious illness.

11. Perhaps the most important single idea we could benefit by is the provision of more employment opportunities for older persons. Japanese older persons are not only permitted, but are expected to continue working or doing housework of some kind as long as they are able. There are special "Talent Banks" to facilitate employment of older workers. There are many ways we could expand job opportunities for older Americans to approach those in

Japan. The 1971 White House Conference on Aging recommended that we earmark a minimum amount of federal manpower funds to improve employment opportunities for older workers; that we vigorously enforce and extend the present legislation against discrimination in employment; that the government become the "employer of last resort" for those older workers unable to find other jobs; and that the government establish a computerized national "job bank" and work-related centers to locate and bring together older persons and potential employers on both a full-time and part-time basis (White House Conference on Aging, pp. 12-15). During the three years following this conference, *none* of these recommendations has been carried out. The Japanese believe that employment of older persons contributes to their physical and mental health, to their life satisfaction, to their financial independence, and to the nation's productivity. There is considerable evidence in Japan and in America that they are correct in this belief.

12. Another idea with potentially great benefit is more integration of older persons in the families of their children and grandchildren. It appears unlikely that Americans will greatly increase the proportions of older persons living with their children. But it may be feasible and desirable for more older Americans to live near enough to their children and grandchildren to contribute more fully to their household activities. On the one side, this would decrease the isolation and inactivity of many older persons, and on the other side it would reduce the parents' burdens of child care, housekeeping, and household maintenance.

13. The Japanese have a nation-wide system of government-supported Elders Clubs, to which about half the elders belong. As we have indicated, these clubs function

not only to provide community service, group study and recreation, but also to provide mutual support and self-pride among the elders. In the United States there are some Senior Citizens Clubs and some get some government support. But compared to Japan, these clubs are few and weak. The National Institute of Senior Aging estimates that less than 5 percent of Americans over 65 belong to any such clubs. If Americans followed Japan's example and established more—and more active—Senior Citizens Clubs, we too could reap the benefits of greatly expanded community service as well as providing opportunities for group study and recreation, mutual support and self-pride to the majority of our older citizens.

14. A related program in Japan is the building of welfare centers for the aged, where various educational, recreational, and consultation services are provided with little or no charge. The centers are subsidized by the government and now exist in most large communities. Again, in America there are a few such centers, but they are rare and usually in precarious financial straits. The 1971 White House Conference on Aging recommended:

In every community and neighborhood, as appropriate, there should be a multi-purpose senior center to provide basic social services, as well as link all older persons to appropriate sources of help, including home-delivered services. The basic services, in clearly identifiable sites, i.e., senior centers, action centers, department of social services, etc., financed as an on-going government program, could be the foundation for such additional services as various levels of government and the voluntary sector, including organizations of the aged, would desire and sponsor (pp. 75).

So far, this recommendation has been implemented in only the larger metropolitan areas, although a few smaller cities are beginning to provide such centers.

15. Perhaps most important in terms of getting these and other recommendations implemented is organized political action and demonstrations by the aged. In Japan, the elders are a recognized political force. This is true not only because they themselves constitute a sizable proportion of the voters, but because they exert a strong influence over the votes of their family and younger friends. Furthermore, because of the high level of organization and self-pride among the elders they are able to mount massive demonstrations and other forms of political pressure to get the government to better meet their needs. There are signs in the United States that more of the aged are beginning to realize the necessity for developing more political "clout." They are joining and working through such organizations as the American Association of Retired Persons and the National Council on the Aging in ever increasing numbers. But massive demonstrations and effective political pressure are still rare. Older Americans could learn from their Japanese counterparts more effective ways of organizing and applying political pressure to improve their situation.

16. Finally, we come to the most complex and yet fundamental way in which we could learn from the Japanese: respect for elders and self-respect among the elders. We have seen how respect for Japanese elders is rooted in the basic social structure of their "vertical society" and in their religion of ancestor worship and filial piety. But the very idea of a vertical society and of ancestor worship would seem alien, if not completely repugnant, to most Americans. Yet it is the main thesis of this book that respect for the aged is the key element which can maintain the status and integration of the aged in modern industrial societies. Therefore, in order to improve the status and integration of

Older Americans, it is necessary to improve our respect for the aged somehow. Instead of the vertical society, perhaps we could use our egalitarian ideology that all persons are entitled to respect because they are humans, regardless of race, sex, *or age*. Instead of ancestor worship, perhaps we could use the Judaic-Christian commandment, "Honor thy father and mother," to increase respect for the aged. Perhaps we could revive the beliefs that "experience is the best teacher" and that knowledge can come from books but only years of experience can provide wisdom. Whatever the method of ideological base, it seems probable that respect for older Americans must be substantially increased before their status and integration will be substantially increased.

In closing, let it be clear that I am not proposing a culture which assumes the aged are superior simply because they are older (as was true in old Japan). Nor am I arguing for a gerontocracy in which the aged have most of the power and rewards of the society (as in ancient Japan). But I do believe we should overcome our stereotypes and prejudices against the aged so that we give them equal respect with all other humans; and I do believe we should stop discriminating against the aged in employment, in our families, and in our communities, so that they can regain an equal share of power and rewards.

Those who agree with these ideals may be able to learn something from the land of "The Honorable Elders."

References

Abegglen, J. *The Japanese Factory.* Glencoe, Ill.: The Free Press, 1958.

Akutagawa, R. *Exotic Japanese Stories.* N. Y.: Liveright Publishing Corp., 1964.

Akutagawa, R. *Japanese Short Stories.* New York: Liveright Publishing Corp., 1961.

Ariyoshi, S. *Kokotsu no Hito (A Man of the Trance).* 1972.

Associated Press. *Almanac 1974.* Maplewood, N. J.: Hammond Almanac, Inc., 1973.

Benedict, R. *The Chrysanthemum and the Sword.* Boston: Houghton Mifflin, 1946.

Beyer, G. and Woods, M. "Living and Activity Patterns of the Aged," Ithaca, N. Y.: Center for Housing and Environmental Studies, Cornell University, 1963.

Bixby, L. "Income of People Aged 65 and Older," *Social Security Bulletin,* 33:4, pp. 3-34, 1970.

Buck, P. *The People of Japan.* New York: Simon and Schuster, 1966.

Cantril, H. *The Patterns of Human Concerns.* New Brunswick, N. J.: Rutgers University Press, 1965.

Cole, R. "Functional Alternatives and Economic Development: An Empirical Example of Permanent Employment in Japan," *American Sociological Review,* 38:4, pp. 424-38 (August 1973).

Cottrell, F. "The Technological and Societal Basis of Aging" in Tibbitts, C. (editor), *Handbook of Social Gerontology.* Chicago: The University of Chicago Press, 1960.

Cowgill, D. and Holmes, L. (editors). *Aging and Modernization.* New York: Appleton-Century-Crofts, 1972.

Cumming, E. and Henry, W. *Growing Old.* New York: Basic Books, 1961.

Drucker, P. "What Can We Learn from Japanese Management," *Harvard Business Review,* 49:2, pp. 110-22, 1971.

Epstein, L. and Murray, J. *The Aged Population of the United States.* Washington: U. S. Government Printing Office, 1967.

Fisher, P. "Major Social Security Issues: Japan, 1972," *Social Security Bulletin,* 36:3, pp. 26-38, 1973.

Gibbs, J. "Suicide," in Merton, R. and Nisbet, R. (editors), *Contemporary Social Problems.* New York: Harcourt, Brace and World, 1966.

Halloran, R. "Elderly Japanese Seeking More Government Help," *The New York Times,* September 16, 1972, pp. 1, 8.

Harris, O. *Japanese Tales of All Ages.* Tokyo: Hokuseido Press, 1937.

Havighurst, R. et al. "Disengagement and Patterns of Aging," in Neugarten, B. (editor), *Middle Age and Aging*. Chicago: The University of Chicago Press, 1968.

Hearn, L. *Japan–An Interpretation*. Rutland, Vt.: Charles E. Tuttle Co., 1955.

Japan Housing Foundation. *Apartment Life and Problems of the Aged*. Tokyo: Japan Housing Foundation, 1973.

Japan Quarterly Editorial Board, *Modern Japanese Short Stories*. Tokyo: Japan Publications, Inc., 1960.

Japan Times, "Filial Piety" (Editorial), *Japan Times*, April 7, 1974, p. 10.

Keene, D. "Basho's Journey to Sarashina," *Transactions of the Asiatic Society of Japan*, series 3, volume 5, 1957.

Keene, D. *Modern Japanese Literature*. N. Y.: Grove Press, 1956.

Koyama, T. *The Changing Social Position of Women in Japan*. Paris: UNESCO, 1961.

Kutner, B. et al. *Five Hundred Over Sixty*. New York: Russell Sage Foundation, 1956.

Metropolitan Life. "Suicide—International Comparisons," *Statistical Bulletin*, Vol. 53, pp. 2-5 (August 1972).

Ministry of Health and Welfare. *Report of the National Survey of the Aged*. Tokyo: Ministry of Health and Welfare, 1960.

Ministry of Health and Welfare. *Survey of the Aged*. Tokyo: Ministry of Health and Welfare, 1970.

Ministry of Health and Welfare. *Material on Old People's Welfare*. Tokyo: Ministry of Health and Welfare, 1971.

Ministry of Health and Welfare. *1971 Survey of Old Persons*. Tokyo: Ministry of Health and Welfare, 1971.

Ministry of Health and Welfare, *Social Welfare Services in Japan, 1972*. Tokyo: Ministry of Health and Welfare, 1972a.

Ministry of Health and Welfare. Summary Results of Survey of the Conditions of Old Persons. Tokyo: Ministry of Health and Welfare (September) 1972b.

Mori, M. *Views on the Welfare of the Aged*. Osaka: Institute for the Study of the Aged, 1973.

Morris, I. (editor). *Modern Japanese Stories*. Rutland, Vt.: Charles E. Tuttle, 1962.

Nakane, C. *Japanese Society*. Berkeley: University of California Press, 1972.

Nasu, S. "The Aged and the Development of Nuclear Families." Tokyo: Metropolitan Institute of Gerontology, 1973.

National Life Center. *Fears About Old Age*. Tokyo: National Life Center, 1972.

Niwa, F. "The Hateful Age," in Morris, I. (editor), *Modern Japanese Stories.* Rutland, Vt.: Charles H. Tuttle Publishing Co., 1972.

Office of the Prime Minister. *Public Opinion Survey about Problems of Old Age.* Tokyo: Office of the Prime Minister, 1973.

Opinion Research Corporation. "The Public Appraises Movies," Princeton, N. J.: Unpublished Survey for Motion Picture Associates of America, 1957.

Palmore, E. "Sociological Aspects of Aging" in Busse, E. and Pfeiffer, E. (editors), *Behavior and Adaptation in Late Life.* Boston: Little Brown and Co., 1969.

Palmore, E. and Jeffers, F. (editors). *Prediction of Life Span.* Lexington, Mass.: D. C. Heath Co., 1971.

Palmore, E. and Whittington, F. "Trends in the Relative Status of the Aged," *Social Forces,* 50:1, pp. 84-90, 1971.

Palmore, E. "Why Do People Retire?" *Aging and Human Development,* Vol. 2, pp. 269-83, 1971.

Palmore, E. "Compulsory Versus Flexible Retirement," *Gerontologist,* 12:4, pp. 343-48, 1972a.

Palmore, E. "Medical Care Needs of the Aged," *Postgraduate Medicine,* 51:5, p. 7, (May and June 1972b).

Palmore, E. and Luikart, C. "Health and Social Factors Related to Life Satisfaction," *Journal of Health and Social Behavior,* 13:68, p. 80, 1972.

Palmore, E. and Manton, K. "Ageism Compared to Racism and Sexism," *Journal of Gerontology,* 28:3, pp. 363-69, 1973.

Palmore, E. and Manton, K. "Modernization and Status of the Aged," *Journal of Gerontology,* 29:2, pp. 205-10, 1974.

Palmore, E. (editor). *Normal Aging II.* Durham, N. C.: Duke University Press, 1974.

Plath, D. "Japan: The After Years," in Cowgill, D. and Holmes, L. (editors), *Aging and Modernization.* New York: Appleton-Century-Crofts, 1972.

Russett, B. *World Handbook of Political and Social Indicators.* New Haven: Yale University Press, 1964.

Shanas, E. and associates. *Old People in Three Industrial Societies.* New York: Atherton Press, 1968.

Silberman, B. *Japanese Character and Culture.* Tucson: The University of Arizona Press, 1962.

Simmons, L. "Aging in Preindustrial Societies," in Tibbits, C. (editor), *Handbook of Social Gerontology.* Chicago: University of Chicago Press, 1960.

Simons, L. *The Role of the Aged in Primitive Society.* London: Oxford University Press, 1945.

Smith, R. "Japan, the Later Years of Life and the Concept of Time," in Kleemeier, R. (editor), *Aging and Leisure*. London: Oxford Univeristy Press, 1961.

Tokyo Metropolitan Government. *Report on Basic Survey of the Aged's Welfare*. Tokyo: Metropolitan Government, 1971.

United Nations. *Demographic Yearbook*, 1963 and 1964. New York: United Nations, 1964 and 1965.

U. S. Bureau of Census. *Statistical Abstract of the U. S., 1973*. Washington: U.S. Government Printing Office, 1973.

United Nations. *Demographic Yearbook*, 1970. New York: United Nations, 1971.

Vogel, E. *Japan's New Middle Class*. Berkeley: University of California Press, 1967.

Weber, M. *The Protestant Ethic and the Spirit of Capitalism*. Parsons, T. (translator). London: Allen and Unwin, 1930.

Welfare Journal. *Problems of Older People*. Tokyo: Welfare Journal Co., 1971.

White House Conference on Aging. *Toward a National Policy on Aging*. Volume II. Washington: U. S. Government Printing Office, 1973.

World Health Organization. Special Subject Report on Suicides. World Health Statistics Report, Volume 21, No. 6. Geneva: World Health Organization, 1968.

Index